William Shakespeare was born in Stratford-upon-Avon in April 1564, and his birth is traditionally celebrated on April 23. The facts of his life, known from surviving documents, are sparse. He was one of eight children born to John Shakespeare, a merchant of some standing in his community. William probably went to the King's New School in Stratford, but he had no university education. In November 1582, at the age of eighteen, he married Anne Hathaway, eight years his senior, who was pregnant with their first child, Susanna. She was born in May 1583. Twins, a boy, Hamnet (who would die at age eleven), and a girl, Judith, were born in 1585. By 1592 Shakespeare had gone to London, working as an actor and already known as a playwright. A rival dramatist, Robert Greene, referred to him as "an upstart crow, beautified with our feathers." Shakespeare became a principal shareholder and playwright of the successful acting troupe, the Lord Chamberlain's Men (later, under James I, called the King's Men). In 1599 the Lord Chamberlain's Men built and occupied the Globe Theatre in Southwark near the Thames River. Here many of Shakespeare's plays were performed by the most famous actors of his time, including Richard Burbage, Will Kempe, and Robert Armin. In addition to his 37 plays, Shakespeare had a hand in others, including *Sir Thomas More* and *The Two Noble Kinsmen*, and he wrote poems, including *Venus and Adonis* and *The Rape of Lucrece*. His 154 sonnets were published, probably without his authorization, in 1609. In 1611 or 1612 he gave up his lodgings in London and devoted more and more of his time to retirement in Stratford, though he continued writing such plays as *The Tempest* and *Henry VIII* until about 1613. He was buried in Holy Trinity Church, Stratford on April 23, 1616. No collected edition of his plays was published during his lifetime, but in 1623 two members of his acting company, John Heminges and Henry Condell, put together the great collection now called the First Folio.

William Shakespeare

THE TEMPEST

Edited by
David Bevington
and
David Scott Kastan

BANTAM CLASSIC

THE TEMPEST
A Bantam Book / published by arrangement with Pearson Education, Inc.

PUBLISHING HISTORY
Scott, Foresman edition published January 1980
Bantam edition, with newly edited text and substantially revised, edited, and
amplified notes, introduction, and other materials / February 1988
Bantam reissue with updated notes, introduction, and other materials /
February 2006

Published by Bantam Dell
A Division of Random House, Inc.
New York, New York

Valuable advice on staging matters has been provided by Richard Hosley
Collations checked by Eric Rasmussen
Additional editorial assistance by Claire McEachern

Book design by Virginia Norey

Library of Congress Catalog Card Number: 87-23194

Bantam Books and the rooster colophon are registered trademarks of
Random House, Inc.

ISBN-10: 0-553-21307-5
ISBN-13: 978-0-553-21307-2

Printed in the United States of America
Published simultaneously in Canada
OPM   28   27   26   25   24

CONTENTS

INTRODUCTION

Shakespeare creates in *The Tempest* a world of the imagination, a place of conflict and ultimately of magical rejuvenation, like the forests of *A Midsummer Night's Dream* and *As You Like It*. The journey to Shakespeare's island is to a realm of art where everything is controlled by the artist figure. Yet the journey is no escape from reality, for the island shows people what they are, as well as what they ought to be. Even its location juxtaposes the "real" world with an idealized landscape: like Plato's New Atlantis or Thomas More's Utopia, Shakespeare's island is to be found both somewhere and nowhere. On the narrative level, it is located in the Mediterranean Sea. Yet there are overtones of the New World, the Western Hemisphere, where Thomas More had situated his island of Utopia. Ariel fetches dew at Prospero's command from the "Bermudas" (1.2.230). Caliban when prostrate reminds Trinculo of a "dead Indian" (2.2.33) who might be displayed before gullible crowds eager to see such a prodigious creature from across the seas, and Caliban's god, Setebos, was, according to Richard Eden's account of Magellan's circumnavigation of the globe (in *History of Travel*, 1577), worshiped by South American natives. An inspiration for Shakespeare's story (for which no direct literary source is known) may well have been various accounts of the shipwreck in the Bermudas in 1609 of the *Sea Venture*, which was carrying settlers to the new Virginian colony. Shakespeare borrowed details from Sylvester Jourdain's *A Discovery of the Bermudas, Otherwise Called the Isle of Devils*, published in 1610, and from William Strachey's *A True Reportory of the Wreck and Redemption . . . from the Islands of the Bermudas*, which Shakespeare must have seen in manuscript since it was not published until after his death. He wrote the play shortly after reading these works, for *The Tempest* was acted at court in 1611. He may also have known or heard of various accounts of Magellan's circumnavigation of the world in 1519–1522 (including Richard Eden's shortened English version, as part of his *History of Travel*, of an Italian narrative by Antonio Pigafetta), Francis Fletcher's journal of Sir Francis Drake's circumnavigation in 1577–1580, Richard Rich's *News from Virginia* (1610), and still other potential sources of information. Shakespeare's fascination with the Western Hemisphere gave him, not the actual location of his story, which remains Mediterranean, but a state of mind associated with newness and the unfamiliar. From this strange and unknown place, we gain a radical perspective on the old world of European culture. Miranda sees on the island a "new world" in which humankind appears "brave" (5.1.185), and, although her wonder must be tempered by Prospero's rejoinder that " 'Tis new to thee" (line 186) and by Aldous Huxley's still more ironic use of her phrase in the title of his satirical novel *Brave New World*, the island endures as a restorative vision. Even though we experience it fleetingly, as in a dream, this nonexistent realm assumes a permanence enjoyed by all great works of art.

Prospero rules autocratically as artist-king and patriarch over this imaginary world, conjuring up trials and visions to test people's intentions and awaken their consciences. To the island come an assortment of persons who, because they require varied ordeals, are separated by Prospero and Ariel into three groups: King Alonso and those accompanying him; Alonso's son, Ferdinand; and Stephano and Trinculo. Prospero's authority over them, though strong, has limits. As Duke of Milan, he was bookishly inattentive to political matters and thus vulnerable to the Machiavellian conniving of his younger brother, Antonio. Only in this world apart, the artist's world, do his powers derived from learning find their proper sphere. Because he cannot control the world beyond his isle, he must wait for "strange, bountiful Fortune, / Now my dear lady" (1.2.179–80) to bring his enemies near his shore. He eschews, moreover, the black arts of diabolism. His is a white magic, devoted ultimately to what he considers moral ends: rescuing Ariel from the spell of the witch

Sycorax, curbing the appetite of Caliban, spying on Antonio and Sebastian in the role of Conscience. He thus comes to see Fortune's gift of delivering his enemies into his hands as an opportunity for him to forgive and restore them, not be revenged.

Such an assumption of godlike power is close to arrogance, even blasphemy, for Prospero is no god. His chief power, learned from books and exercised through Ariel, is to control the elements so as to create illusion—of separation, of death, of the gods' blessing. Yet, since he is human, even this power is an immense burden and temptation. Prospero has much to learn, like those whom he controls. He must subdue his anger, his self-pity, his readiness to blame others, his domineering over Miranda. He must overcome the vengeful impulse he experiences toward those who have wronged him, and he must conquer the longing many a father feels to hold on to his daughter when she is desired by another man. He struggles with these problems through his art, devising games and shows in which his angry self-pity and jealousy are transmuted into playacting scenes of divine warning and forgiveness toward his enemies and watchful parental austerity toward Miranda and Ferdinand. Prospero's responsibilities cause him to behave magisterially and to be resented by the spirits of the isle. His authority is problematic to us because he seems so patriarchal, colonialist, even sexist and racist in his arrogating to himself the right and responsibility to control others in the name of values they may not share. Ariel longs to be free of this authority. Perhaps our sympathy for Prospero is greatest when we perceive that he, too, with mixed feelings of genuine relief and melancholy, is ready to lay aside his demanding and self-important role as creative moral intelligence.

Alonso and his court party variously illustrate the unregenerate world left behind in Naples and Milan. We first see them on shipboard, panicky and desperate, their titles and finery mocked by roaring waves. Futile ambition seems destined for a watery demise. Yet death by water in this play is a transfiguration rather than an end, a mystical rebirth, as in the regenerative cycle of the seasons from winter to summer. Ariel suggests as much in his song about a drowned father: "Those are pearls that were his eyes. / Nothing of him that doth fade / But doth suffer a sea change / Into something rich and strange" (1.2.402–5). Still, this miracle is not apparent at first to those who are caught in the illusion of death. As in T. S. Eliot's *The Waste Land*, which repeatedly alludes to *The Tempest*, self-blinded human beings fear a disaster that is ironically the prelude to reawakening.

The illusions created on the island serve to test these imperfect men and to make them reveal their true selves. Only Gonzalo, who long ago aided Prospero and Miranda when they were banished from Milan, responds affirmatively to illusion. In his eyes, their having been saved from drowning is a miracle: they breathe fresh air, the grass is green on the island, and their very garments appear not to have been stained by the salt water. His ideal commonwealth (2.1.150–71), which Shakespeare drew in part from an essay by Montaigne, postulates a natural goodness in humanity and makes no allowance for the darker propensities of human behavior, but at least Gonzalo's cheerfulness is in refreshing contrast to the jaded sneers of some of his companions. Sebastian and Antonio react to the magic isle, as to Gonzalo's commonwealth, by cynically refusing to believe in miracles. They scoff at Gonzalo for insistently looking on the bright side; if he were to examine his supposedly unstained clothes more carefully, they jest, he would discover that his pockets are filled with mud. Confident that they are unobserved, they seize the opportunity afforded by Alonso's being asleep to plot a murder and political coup. This attempt is not only despicable but also madly ludicrous, for they are all shipwrecked and no longer have kingdoms over which to quarrel. Even more ironically, Sebastian and Antonio, despite their insolent belief in their self-sufficiency, are being observed. The villains must be taught that an unseen power keeps track of their misdeeds. However presumptuous Prospero may be to assume through Ariel's means the role of godlike observer, he does awaken conscience and prevent murder. The villains may revert to type when returned to their usual habitat, but even they are at least briefly moved to an awareness of the unseen (3.3.21–7). Alonso, more worthy than they, though burdened, too, with sin, responds to his situation with guilt and despair, for he assumes that his son Ferdinand's death is the just punishment of the gods for Alonso's part in the earlier overthrow of Prospero. Alonso must be led, by means of curative illusions, through the purgative experience of contrition to the reward he thinks impossible and undeserved: reunion with his lost son.

Alonso is thus, like Posthumus in *Cymbeline* or Leontes in *The Winter's Tale*, a tragicomic figure—sinful, contrite, forgiven. Alonso's son Ferdinand must also undergo ordeals and visions devised by Prospero to test his worth, but more on the level of romantic comedy. Ferdinand is young, innocent, and hopeful, well matched to Miranda. From the start, Prospero obviously approves of his prospective son-in-law. Yet even Prospero, needing to prepare himself for a life in which Miranda will no longer be solely his, is not ready to lay aside at least the comic fiction of parental opposition. He invents difficulties, imposes tasks of log-bearing (like those assigned Caliban), and issues stern warnings against premarital lust. In the comic mode, parents are expected to cross their children in matters of the heart. Prospero is so convincing in his role of overbearing parent, insisting on absolute unthinking obedience from his daughter, that we remain unsure whether he is truly like that or whether we are meant to sense in his performance a grappling with his own deepest feelings of possessiveness and autocratic authority, tempered finally by his awareness of the arbitrariness of such a role and his readiness to let Miranda decide for herself. As a teacher of youth, moreover, Prospero is convinced by long experience that prizes too easily won are too lightly esteemed. Manifold are the temptations urging Ferdinand to surrender to the natural rhythms of the isle as Caliban would. In place of ceremonies conducted in civilized societies by the church, Prospero must create the illusion of ceremony by his art. The betrothal of Ferdinand and Miranda accordingly unites the best of both worlds: the natural innocence of the island, which teaches them to avoid the corruptions of civilization at its worst, and the higher law of nature achieved through moral wisdom at its best. To this marriage, the goddesses Iris, Ceres, and Juno bring promises of bounteous harvest, "refreshing showers," celestial harmony, and a springtime brought back to the earth by Proserpina's return from Hades (4.1.76–117). In Ferdinand and Miranda, "nurture" is wedded to "nature." This bond unites spirit and flesh, legitimizing erotic pleasure by incorporating it within Prospero's vision of a cosmic moral order.

At the lowest level of this traditional cosmic and moral framework, in Prospero's view, are Stephano and Trinculo. Their comic scenes juxtapose them with Caliban, for he represents untutored Nature, whereas they represent the unnatural depths to which human beings brought up in civilized society can fall. In this they resemble Sebastian and Antonio, who have learned in supposedly civilized Italy arts of intrigue and political murder. The antics of Stephano and Trinculo burlesque the conduct of their presumed betters, thereby exposing to ridicule the self-deceptions of ambitious men. The clowns desire to exploit the natural wonders of the isle by taking Caliban back to civilization to be shown in carnivals or by plying him with strong drink and whetting his resentment against authority. These plottings are in vain, however, for, like Sebastian and Antonio, the clowns are being watched. The clowns teach Caliban to cry out for "freedom" (2.2.184), by which they mean license to do as one pleases, but are foiled by Ariel as comic nemesis. Because they are degenerate buffoons, Prospero as satirist devises for them an exposure that is appropriately humiliating and satirical.

In contrast with them, Caliban is in many ways a sympathetic character. His sensitivity to natural beauty, as in his descriptions of the "nimble marmoset" or the dreaming music he so often hears (2.2.168; 3.2.137–45), is entirely appropriate to this child of nature. He is, to be sure, the child of a witch and is called many harsh names by Miranda and Prospero, such as "Abhorrèd slave" and "a born devil, on whose nature / Nurture can never stick" (1.2.354; 4.1.188–9). Yet he protests with some justification that the island was his in the first place and that Prospero and Miranda are interlopers. His very existence calls radically into question the value of civilization, which has shown itself capable of limitless depravity. What profit has Caliban derived from learning Prospero's language other than, as he puts it, to "know how to curse" (1.2.367)? With instinctive cunning, he senses that books are his chief enemy and plots to destroy them first in his attempt at rebellion. The unspoiled natural world does indeed offer civilization a unique perspective on itself. In this it resembles Gonzalo's ideal commonwealth, which, no matter how laughably implausible from the cynic's point of view, does at least question some assumptions—economic, political, and social—common in Western societies.

Radical perspectives of this kind invite consideration of many unsettling questions about exploration, colonialist empire building, and sexual imperialism. The fleeting comparison of Caliban to an indigenous native (2.2.33), although ignored in stage productions of the play until the late nineteenth century, suggests a discourse on colonialism in *The Tempest* that anticipates to a remarkable degree a doleful history of exploitation, of providing rum and guns to the natives, and of taking away land through violent expropriation in the name of bringing civilization and God to the New World. Stephano and Trinculo, pouring wine down Caliban's throat and thus reducing him to a worshiping slave, show exploitation at its worst, but surely the play allows us to wonder also if Prospero's enslavement of Caliban, however high-minded in its claims of preventing disorder and rape, is not tainted by the same imperatives of possession and control. The issue is wonderfully complex. Caliban is a projection of both the naturally depraved savage described in many explorers' accounts and the nobly innocent savage described by Montaigne. By dramatizing the conflict without taking sides, Shakespeare leaves open a debate about the worth of Prospero's endeavor to contain Caliban's otherness and produces an ambivalent result in which the apparent victory of colonialism and censorship does not entirely conceal the contradictory struggle through which those values are imposed. The play's many open-ended questions apply not only to the New World but also, nearer at hand, to Ireland—an island on the margins of Britain that was regarded as both savage and threatening.

The play's discourse also raises issues of class and political justice. The battle between Prospero and Caliban is one of "master" and "man" (2.2.183); even if Caliban's cry of "freedom" leads him only into further enslavement by Stephano and Trinculo (who are themselves masterless men), the play does not resolve the conflict by simply reimposing social hierarchy. Caliban, Stephano, and Trinculo are all taught a lesson and are satirically punished for their rebellious behavior, but Caliban at least is pardoned and is left behind on the island at the play's end where presumably he will no longer be a slave. In political terms, Prospero resolves the long-standing hostilities between Milan and Naples by his astute arranging of the betrothal of Miranda to Ferdinand. However much it is idealized as a romantic match presided over harmoniously by the gods, it is also a political union aimed at bringing together the ruling families of those two city-states. Prospero's masque, his ultimate vision of the triumph of civilization, transforms the myth of the rape of a daughter (Proserpina) in such a way as to preserve the daughter's chaste honor in a union that will repair the political and social damage done by the ouster of Prospero from his dukedom of Milan. For these reasons, the betrothal of Ferdinand and Miranda must have seemed politically relevant to Shakespeare's audience when *The Tempest* was performed before King James at Whitehall in November of 1611 and then again at court in 1613 in celebration of the marriage of James's daughter Elizabeth to Frederick, the Elector Palatine.

The play's ending is far from perfectly stable. Antonio never repents, and we cannot be sure what the island will be like once Prospero has disappeared from the scene. Since Prospero's occupation of the island replicates in a sense the process by which he himself was overthrown, we cannot know when the cycle of revolution will ever cease. We cannot even be sure of the extent to which Shakespeare is master of his own colonial debate in *The Tempest* or, conversely, the extent to which today we should feel ourselves free to relativize, ironize, or in other ways criticize this

play for apparent or probable prejudices. Not even a great author like Shakespeare can escape the limits of his own time, any
more than we can escape the limits of our own. Perhaps we can
nonetheless project ourselves, as spectators and readers, into
Shakespeare's attempt to celebrate humanity's highest achieve-
ment in the union of the island with the civilized world.
Miranda and Ferdinand have bright hopes for the future, even if
those hopes must be qualified by Prospero's melancholic observation that the "brave new world" with "such people in't" is
only "new to thee," to those who are young and not yet experi-
enced in the world's vexations. Even Caliban may be at last rec-
onciled to Prospero's insistent idea of a harmony between will
and reason, no matter how perilously and delicately achieved.
Prospero speaks of Caliban as a "thing of darkness I / Acknowledge
mine," and Caliban vows to "be wise hereafter / And seek for
grace" (5.1.278–9, 298–9). Prospero's view is that the natural
human within is more contented, better understood, and more
truly free when harmonized with reason.

Caliban is a part of humanity; Ariel is not. Ariel can com-
prehend what compassion and forgiveness would be like, "were I
human" (5.1.20), and can take good-natured part in Prospero's
designs to castigate or reform his fellow mortals, but Ariel longs
to be free in quite another sense from that meant by Caliban.
Ariel takes no part in the final integration of human society.
This spirit belongs to a magic world of song, music, and illusion
that the artist borrows for his use but that exists eternally outside of him. Like the elements of air, earth, fire, and water in
which it mysteriously dwells, this spirit is morally neutral but in-
credibly vital. From it the artist achieves powers of imagination,
enabling him to bedim the noontide sun or call forth the dead
from their graves. These visions are illusory in the profound
sense that all life is illusory, an "insubstantial pageant" melted
into thin air (4.1.150–5). Prospero the artist cherishes his own
humanity, as a promise of surcease from his labors. Yet the arti-
fact created by the artist endures, existing apart from time and
place, as does Ariel: "Then to the elements / Be free, and fare
thou well!" (5.1.321–2). No doubt it is a romantic fiction to

associate the dramatist Shakespeare with Prospero's farewell to his art, but it is an almost irresistible idea, because we are so moved by the sense of completion and yet humility, the exultation and yet the calm contained in this leave taking.

As though to demonstrate the summation of his artistry as magician-poet in what he may indeed have designed as his farewell to the stage, Shakespeare puts on a dazzling display of the verbal artistry for which he had already become famous. His command of blank verse is, by this time, more flexible and protean than ever before, with a marked increase in run-on lines, caesuras in mid line, the sharing of blank verse lines between two or more speakers, feminine endings, and other features of the late Shakespearean style. The play is notable for its bravura passages, such as those that begin "Our revels now are ended" (4.1.148–58) and "Ye elves of hills" (5.1.33–57). With its opening storm scene and its solemn shows and masques—the *"several strange shapes"* bringing in a banquet and the appearance of Ariel *"like a harpy"* in 3.3, the masque of Iris, Ceres, and Juno in 4.1, and Prospero's confining the Neapolitans to a charmed circle in 5.1—*The Tempest* presents itself as a tour de force of spectacle and grandeur in which all of these dazzling events are also astutely interrupted by the resurgence of human appetite and by satiric correction. At every turn the drama manifests a deft compression of time and event. The tone is masterfully assured, in prose as in verse. Images of a dreamlike world come together in a remarkable amalgam whereby the characters participate in a fluid world that moves through them even as they move through it, becoming one with the tempest of time.

THE TEMPEST
ON STAGE

Mark Twain once joked that Shakespeare's plays were not by Shakespeare but by another author of the same name. His joke might, with a slight alteration, be applied to the performance history of *The Tempest*. Something called *The Tempest* has never failed to delight audiences, but from the mid-seventeenth until the late eighteenth century what audiences saw was truly another play of the same name. Adaptation began shortly after Shakespeare's death, if not before. His own play had been acted before King James by Shakespeare's acting company, the King's Men, on November 1, 1611, and in the winter of 1612–1613 "before the Princess' Highness the Lady Elizabeth and the Prince Palatine Elector" in honor of their betrothal. Scholars have argued, though without much evidence, that Shakespeare composed the masque in act 4 especially for this occasion; if he did, the process of musical elaboration began early and with his own imprimatur. More likely, the short play we have, masque and all, was written to be acted in late 1611 and afterward at the Globe Theatre, at the Blackfriars playhouse, and at court when the King so wished. Dr. Simon Forman, who recorded in his journal that he saw *Cymbeline* and *The Winter's Tale* in 1611, does not mention *The Tempest*. In any event, the King's Men were soon performing a fanciful reply to Shakespeare's play, by John Fletcher, called *The Sea Voyage* (1622), and in 1667 the theater in Lincoln's Inn Fields, London, staged a production of *The Tempest* as altered by William Davenant and John Dryden.

This version of *The Tempest* was a great success. Diarist Samuel Pepys saw it eight times between 1667 and 1669, more times than any other Shakespeare play he saw except *Macbeth*, and bestowed on it his warmest praise: in January of 1669 he wrote that he "could not be more pleased almost in a comedy," and later that same year he declared it "the most innocent play that ever I saw." The authors' success lay in appealing to the tastes of their age for symmetry. Davenant hit on the idea that Shakespeare's story of a young woman (Miranda) who has never seen a man could be paired with that of a young man who has never seen a woman. "By this means," wrote Davenant afterward, "those two characters of innocence and love might the more illustrate and commend each other."

The added counterplot is thus a mirror of the main plot. Long ago, the story goes, Prospero brought with him to the island the young Duke of Mantua, named Hippolito, and has kept him secluded in a remote cave where, improbably enough, he has never seen Miranda—or her sister Dorinda. When Hippolito does see Dorinda for the first time, in a scene that parallels Miranda's first encounter with Ferdinand, Hippolito's male response is to want her and all beautiful women besides, and so he quarrels with Ferdinand and is seemingly killed by him. For this offense Ferdinand is condemned to death by Prospero, until Hippolito is revived by Ariel's aid and goes on to join the other three lovers in a predictable contretemps of jealousies and misplaced affections. Caliban, meanwhile, has a sister, Sycorax, and Ariel has a fellow-spirit named Milcha. The broadly comic plot of Stephano, Trinculo, and Caliban is enlarged into a quarrel for royal supremacy among Stephano, Mustacho, and Ventoso on the one hand and Trincalo (i.e., Trinculo), Caliban, and Sycorax on the other, with pointed satirical application to the recent factionalism of England's mid-century civil war.

With its many songs, Shakespeare's *The Tempest* was an obvious candidate for operatic treatment. Thomas Shadwell's *The Tempest* (produced in 1673, published the following year) retains the plot symmetries of Davenant and Dryden, including the topical satire directed at civil strife, while adding substantially to the music and spectacle. Shadwell gives an enlarged part to Milcha so that she and Ariel can sing together and dance a saraband. At the dramatic moment when Prospero sets Ariel and then Milcha free, "both fly up and cross in the air." When Ariel sings "Come unto these yellow sands," as in Shakespeare (1.2.378–390), Milcha answers with "Full fathom five" (ll.400–407). Together they sing an added song, "Dry those tears which are o'erflowing." The musical settings by Pietro Reggio, Matthew Locke, and Pelham Humphrey were of a high order, and the standard remained high when, later in the century, the songs were reset to music by Henry Purcell and others.

Scenic and musical splendor prevails everywhere in Shadwell's opera. It opens with an overture, a rising curtain, and the discovery of a noble arched frontispiece supported by Corinthian columns wreathed in roses. Several Cupids fly about them. The allegorical figure of Fame appears; angels hold the royal arms of England. Behind the arch lies the menacing scene, a sky darkened by storm clouds, a coast strewn with rocks, a troubled sea in continual motion. Frightful spirits fly among the terrorized sailors. When the ship begins to sink, "the whole house is darkened, and a shower of fire falls upon 'em"—presumably the sailors, not the audience. Lightning flashes and thunder sounds. Thereupon, "in the midst of the shower of fire, the scene changes. The cloudy sky, rocks, and sea vanish, and, when the lights return, discover that beautiful part of the island which was the habitation of Prospero. 'Tis composed of three walks of cypress trees. Each sidewalk leads to a cave, in one of which Prospero keeps his daughters, in the other Hippolito. The middle walk is of great depth, and leads to an open part of the island." Possibly the effect of darkness was achieved by the shutting of flats (theatrical scenery), or the removal and then return of hanging candle-fixtures, or both.

Later in the opera, according to the contemporary account of John Downes, the audience sees one of Ariel's spirits "flying away with a table furnished out with fruits, sweetmeats, and all sorts of viands, just when Duke Trinculo and his companions were going to dinner." A masque of Furies, introduced by Dryden in 1667, is much enlarged by Shadwell with allegorical figures such as Pride, Fraud, Rapine, and Murder. A concluding masque of Neptune and Amphitrite shows these sea gods, along with Oceanus and Tethys, arising "in a chariot drawn with sea-horses," while Tritons and Nereides sport at their side. A dance of twelve Tritons is followed by a scene at sunrise in which Ariel, accompanied by other spirits, flies from the sun toward the spectators and hovers in the air while speaking the last lines. In Shadwall's hands *The Tempest* has become the embodiment of the seventeenth-century courtly masque, complete with anti-masque in the ludicrous antics of Stephano and Trinculo.

The Davenant-Dryden and Shadwell adaptations, or variations of them, held the stage for much of the eighteenth century. At the Theatre Royal, Drury Lane, there were over 180 performances in the first half of the century alone. A revival of *The Tempest*—or *The Enchanted Island*, as the adaptation was also known—in 1706 included a masque composed by "the late Mr. Henry Purcell." A revival in 1712 was again a great success; according to actor-manager Colly Cibber, the production achieved "the greatest profit that in so little a time had yet been known in my memory." In 1715 Drury Lane produced a similar version "with the tempest, with scenes, machines, dances, and all the original decorations proper to the play," in response to a revival of Beaumont and Fletcher's popular *The Island Princess* at the theater in Lincoln's Inn Fields, London. When money could not be found for the Shadwell extravaganza, Davenant and Dryden's adaptation filled in. Although James Lacy claimed to produce the play at Drury Lane in 1746 "as written by Shakespeare, never acted there before," he in fact added Shadwell's elaborate masque of Neptune and Amphitrite in act 5, and at all events the theater soon returned to Davenant and Dryden. Actor-manager David Garrick produced *The Tempest: An Opera, Taken from Shakespeare* in 1756 at Drury Lane, without Hippolito and Dorinda but with Davenant's added clowns. John Christopher Smith, a protégé of Handel, composed the opera, with some thirty-two songs, duets, and a trio for Trinculo, Stephano, and Ventoso. Sixty children presented a garland dance at the end of act 2, and subsequently there was a pantomime of Fortunatus, or the Genii. Garrick did revive Shakespeare's play in 1757 with Henry Mossop as Prospero and Hannah Pritchard as Miranda, albeit with some heavy cutting in act 2, scene 1, and this version enjoyed sixty-one performances before Garrick retired in 1776.

We get a clear impression of costuming and setting during this period from a contemporary engraving seemingly based on De Loutherbourg's designs for a 1777 production at Drury Lane. Ferdinand is in the powdered wig and elegant attire of an eighteenth-century gentleman, Miranda in a sweeping coiffure with outfit to match. Such costuming evidently did not seem out of keeping with the spectacle of the Davenant-Dryden-Shadwell tradition, which continued only somewhat abated. John Philip Kemble, in his 1789 revival at Drury Lane, sought "to admit in a temperate way the additions of Dryden," retaining the Hippolito-Dorinda plot though eliminating Milcha, Sycorax, Ventoso, and Mustacho. Kemble added music in 1789, including a duet for Ferdinand and Miranda, though he cut it back in subsequent years. He cast an actress as Hippolito. In staging effects, Kemble continued the focus on the shipwreck, transferring it to the beginning of act 2 with the following directions: "The sea. A ship in a tempest. Spirits of the wind dancing. Chorus by spirits of the storm. The ship seems to founder. Ariel and all the other spirits disappear." At the play's end, Prospero waves his wand and the scene vanishes, discovering "a view of a calm sea, and the King's ship riding at anchor . . . Ariel and the spirits re-ascend into the sky." The Haymarket Theatre, not to be outdone, staged a ballet of *The Enchanted Island* in 1804 that went beyond the effects called for by Kemble. In 1806, Kemble, who had by this time moved to the Theatre Royal, Covent Garden, produced the play there, retaining the tradition of spectacular staging but reducing the operatic content. This version of the play became the standard acting version in the first third of the nineteenth century. Kemble's own performance as Prospero was well received, even though he was criticized for his controversial decision to pronounce "aches" in the Elizabethan manner as "aitches."

The Tempest offered many temptations to the theater manager predisposed toward musical and visual elaboration, and nineteenth-century managers, with their growing fondness for scenic *vraisemblance*, made few attempts to resist. Frederic Reynolds and H. R. Bishop brought out an operatic version in 1821 at Covent Garden "as altered and adapted by Dryden and Davenant." The musical score borrowed not only from Purcell but from Haydn, Mozart, Rossini, and others. William Charles Macready played Prospero and John Emery played Caliban, while most other parts were assigned to singers. The scenes included Prospero's cave, the interior of the island, a rocky part of the island, Hippolito's cave, a lake and mountains by moonlight, a volcanic mountain and lake, and finally a cave that changes to the last scene. Caliban gave the appearance of "a hairy man of the woods"; Ariel, portrayed as feminine, had painted gauze wings. The chorus singers in the finale came down from the ceiling on wires.

Macready, after playing Prospero in this 1821 production and also in Alfred Bunn's revival at Drury Lane in 1833 as "altered by Dryden and Davenant," brought out his own The Tempest in 1838 at Covent Garden with a restored Shakespeare text but still with a female Ariel (played by Priscilla Horton) suspended in the air while she sang and wearing a diaphanous long gown and fairy wings. Macready took out the dialogue of the first scene to allow room for a spectacular storm. When Ferdinand drew his sword on Prospero but was prevented by Prospero's spell from doing harm with it (1.2), the young man's sword was made to fly off over his head. Helen Faucit played Miranda. Macready had at last brought an end to the long reign of Davenant and Dryden, but the resort to scenic effects was destined to continue for some time.

A Covent Garden revival of 1842, again by Macready, opened with a huge sea vessel, fully rigged and manned, and tossing about on a tempestuous ocean. "The size of the ship," wrote the reviewer for *John Bull*, "and the ingenuity with which it was managed, now rising so as to discover the keel and then dipping to the level of the stage, seeming to sink into the mimic waters, rendered the effect particularly real." Samuel Phelps, at the Sadler's Wells Theatre in 1847, similarly used spectacular effects: a full-scale ship was battered in the opening storm, its mast struck by a fireball. Phelps's own performance as Prospero was widely praised, and the production itself was hailed by the reviewer for *The Times* as the "best combination of Shakespeare and scenery." Influenced by Phelps's success, the Surrey Theatre produced *The Tempest* in 1853 with "dioramic and pictorial illusion of a storm and wreck," masques, dances, and mechanical effects. Even in America the impact of Phelps was felt. William Burton's production in 1854 in New York followed Macready in restoring Shakespeare's text to the stage, but its spectacular theatrical effects were largely inspired by Phelps.

Charles Kean's *The Tempest* of 1857 at the Princess's Theatre may have reached some sort of pinnacle in spectacular staging. The deck actually tossed and pitched during the storm scene and appeared to founder with all on board, whereupon the storm dispersed, allowing the sun to rise on the island where Prospero (Kean), accompanied by Miranda, stood on a rock and supervised the calming of the waters. In act 3, a scene of desolation changed suddenly into a tropical paradise, with trees rising from the earth, fountains and waterfalls flowing from the rocks, and nymphs and satyrs bearing fruit and flowers. In an allegorical finale, Prospero released the spirits who had aided him in his art and then delivered the epilogue from the deck of a vessel that sailed off into the distance, leaving Ariel alone and suspended in air. A distant chorus of spirits accompanied the fall of the curtain. Throughout, Ariel took the various forms of a ball of fire, a delicate creature arising from a tuft of flowers, a water nymph on the back of a dolphin, or a spirit riding on a bat. Kean, in other words, literalized the words of Shakespeare's song, "Where the bee sucks, there suck I. / In a cowslip's bell I lie; / There I couch when owls do cry. / On the bat's back I do fly" (5.1.88–91). Little could be added in this vein by Frank Benson at the Lyceum Theatre in 1900 or by Herbert Beerbohm Tree at His Majesty's in 1904, though they certainly did their best.

The modern stage thus had a clear mandate for change: to free *The Tempest* from a spectacular tradition that was not only costly and inflexible, requiring cuts and rearrangements of the text to accommodate the scenery, but also was ready to visualize externally and superficially what Shakespeare's own theater leaves to the imagination. A return to a theater in which stage image can suggest conflicts and the characters' states of mind, rather than literalize, was long overdue.

The inevitability of the change can in fact be sensed in the last years of the nineteenth century. In part because of a tight budget, Frank Benson's production at Stratford-upon-Avon in 1891 began the movement away from the lavish stage traditions of Phelps and Kean. Benson cut the opening shipwreck and in general simplified the play's staging (though he did add a fanciful entrance for Ferdinand "drawn by a silver thread, held by two tiny Cupids"). Benson's version was regularly revived over the next quarter-century, and his own performance as Caliban was enormously influential. Benson based his interpretation of the character on a book by Daniel Wilson, Professor of History and English Literature at the University of Toronto, who argued that Shakespeare's Caliban is the missing link that Darwinian evolutionary theory demands. The athletic Benson, dressed in a costume his wife described as "half monkey, half cocoanut," climbed trees, hung upside down, and carried an actual fish.

The two significant aspects of Benson's production, the simplified staging and the emphasis upon Caliban, were to exert a significant impact upon subsequent performances of the play. William Poel and the Elizabethan Stage Society performed the play in 1897 on an open stage with limited scenery and without scene shifts. The elaborate music of the operatic *Tempests* gave way to a simple score for pipe and tabor by Arnold Dolmetsch, leading George Bernard Shaw to rejoice in Poel's decision to "leave to the poet the work of conjuring up the isle 'full of noises, sounds, and sweet airs.'"

In 1904, Herbert Beerbohm Tree tried to recapture the visual splendor of the lavish nineteenth-century productions. "Of all of Shakespeare's works," wrote Tree, "*The Tempest* is probably the one which most demands the aid of modern stagecraft." But if his elaborate lighting effects and his extensive use of pantomime and ballet pointed back to—and brought to an end—the tradition of spectacular staging, his portrayal of Caliban as thoughtful and sensitive looked forward to the shifting emphasis of modern productions that would increasingly see Caliban as less demonic and more tragic than earlier productions allowed and would recognize Prospero's power as more problematic. Tree's version ended with a final tableau of Caliban on the shore reaching out "in mute despair" to the departing ship.

In 1914 Ben Greet brought his production, previously on tour in England and America, to London's Old Vic. Greet followed the new tradition of simplified staging, using "no special scenery" but introducing background music by Arthur Sullivan. Sybil Thorndike, who in America had played Ceres, now took the role of Ferdinand. Two years later in New York, John Corbin and Louis Calvert produced the play at the Century Theater "in the manner of the Elizabethan stage." The text was presented "in its full integrity" and every effort was made to reproduce the full range of staging possibilities offered by Shakespeare's theater. Corbin criticized Poel and Greet for an impoverished conception of these possibilities, maintaining that Shakespeare's company inevitably would have dressed its actors in lavish costumes and made use of spectacular "flyings." "There is no reason to suppose," he argued, "that the public theatres would neglect an effect so striking." Though some reviewers criticized the production as merely an "archaeological experiment" devoid of any theatrical ingenuity, others praised Corbin's reconstruction for its quick pacing, which permitted "the fine full text of Shakespeare's play [to] unfold rapidly without long, tedious, disillusioning waits between scenes."

The growing effort to understand the conditions of Shakespeare's theater led William Bridges-Adams in 1919 to produce his revival at Stratford-upon-Avon as the play might have been done at court. He used a gauze drop curtain with the portraits and coats-of-arms of the Princess Elizabeth and the

Elector Palatine for whose betrothal *The Tempest* had been performed at court in 1612–1613. Though the production attempted to reproduce the pageantry of the Jacobean masque, it used only a simple set of movable, bare platforms, seeking its stateliness in speech and movement.

At the Old Vic in 1930 Harcourt Williams directed John Gielgud as Prospero, Ralph Richardson as Caliban, and Leslie French as Ariel (the first male to play the role since 1734). Ten years later at the Old Vic, Gielgud again played Prospero, this time in a production by George Devine and Marius Goring. Gielgud's Prospero was anxious and ironic. Goring's Ariel, as Audrey Williamson wrote, was "not cruel, but cool and remote," while Jack Hawkins's Caliban "vividly suggested the slow groping towards humanity." In 1957 Peter Brook directed Gielgud in his third *Tempest*. Increasingly Gielgud's interpretations of Prospero, as they moved from benign serenity to brooding irritability, revealed the price Prospero pays for his power, and Brook's production continued the movement away from the innocent theatrical magic of the stage tradition and toward an exploration of the tensions and ambiguities discovered in the text. The island was dark, overgrown with vegetation, a projection of Prospero's tortured mind, and Gielgud was an embittered anchorite determined on revenge.

Brook returned to the play in 1968 at London's Roundhouse Theatre in an experimental version commissioned by Jean-Louis Barrault using French, Japanese, English, and American actors to explore the very nature of theater. Gielgud returned to *The Tempest* for a fourth time in 1974 at the National Theatre. Directed by Peter Hall, this production, like that of Bridges-Adams in 1919, conceived of the play as a Jacobean masque, but unlike the earlier production it understood the masque not as mere royal pageantry but as an expression of royal authority. Gielgud's Prospero was, in Hall's words, "a man of power, of intelligence, as shrewd and cunning and egocentric as Churchill." Costumed like the Elizabethan astrologer John Dee, Gielgud's Prospero exerted his power over a Caliban (played by Denis

Quilley) who was made up to be half monster and half noble savage.

The benign magician of the early stage history of the play has given way to something more interesting and complex. In Jonathan Miller's 1970 production at London's Mermaid Theatre the play's colonial themes were explicitly explored. Basing his conception on Dominique O. Mannoni's account of the 1947 revolution in Madagascar, *La Psychologie de la Colonisation* (published in English as *Prospero and Caliban* in 1953), Miller had two black actors, Norman Beaton and Rudolph Walker, play Ariel and Caliban, clarifying the colonial parable that he found in the play. Beaton's Ariel was a noble African who successfully internalized the skills of his master, while Walker's Caliban was a demoralized and degraded slave. Miller's production ended with Ariel eagerly picking up the staff Prospero has discarded and Caliban shaking his fist in fury at the departing ship.

Among the most remarkable modern productions of *The Tempest* was one that heroically resisted the disillusionment that has characterized so many recent versions even as it recognized the play as a play of failure—the failure of the dream of perfectibility. Performed first in Milan in 1977, revived in 1982, and brought to America for the Olympic Arts Festival in Los Angeles in 1984, Giorgio Strehler's *La Tempesta* (translated into Italian by Agostino Lombardo) represented an extraordinary triumph of theatrical illusion. Prospero's relationship with Ariel was at the center of Strehler's understanding of the play, a resonant metaphor for the relationship of the director and the actor. Until the end, Ariel, a commedia dell'arte Pierrot, was attached to a wire, soaring in the air, sometimes landing nimbly on Prospero's raised finger, yet always unable to escape Prospero's will. When at last he was released, he stumbled on shaky legs, exiting through the audience. Prospero's epilogue became an apology for the limitations of his magic and for the limitations of the theater itself. As he came before the audience, the simple set suddenly disassembled, revealing the bareness and artifice of the theater's illusions. With the audience's applause, the set reformed and Ariel returned to Prospero's side. Strehler's innovative production achieved the theatrical magic that the play demands, thereby offering a profound and moving investigation of the power of theater itself. "In this *Tempest*," Strehler wrote, "we have felt the fallible, desperate, triumphant grandeur and responsibility of our profession."

More recent productions continued to explore the ways the play's self-conscious theatricality intersects with other concerns. In 1995, at the New York Shakespeare Festival in Central Park (and moving that fall to the Broadhurst Theater on Broadway), George Wolfe directed a colorful, inventive *Tempest* set in some unspecific exotic locale. Brazilian stilt-walkers, Kabuki masks, Indonesian shadow play, and puppets established the theme of the clash of European culture with the wide world it had become aware of and was trying to dominate. A female Ariel and a monstrous Caliban were played by African American actors (Aunjanue Ellis and Teagle F. Bougere), and their relations with Prospero and Miranda were clearly designed to suggest the experience of slaves. The production was dominated by Patrick Stewart's angry, often frustrated, and finally exhausted Prospero, who with some obvious relief came before the audience to ask its acceptance. As he accepted the fact that now his "charms are all o'erthrown" (Epilogue), the body mike used for outdoor amplification suddenly shut off, revealing how much this is a play not least about the stage-magic of playing.

In the summer of 1993 in Stratford-upon-Avon (and then the following summer at London's Barbican Theatre), Sam Mendes directed the play as a succession of theatrical illusions, beginning with the opening on a bare stage with only a large basket. As the house lights darkened, Ariel (Simon Russell Beale) emerged from the basket, climbed on top of it, and beckoned to the flies for a lantern to descend to him, which he pushed to make it swing. Beale was far from the ethereal Ariels of most productions. Physically formidable, he had no interest in Prospero's affection, and when freed at the end he spat in the Duke's face, exiting through a door in the back wall, which he closed firmly behind him, leaving Prospero very much alone as he faced the audience for his epilogue. Alec McCowen's

Prospero was self-righteous and quick-tempered, seemingly enjoying his power over the Italian courtiers. Still, the magic of this production, and arguably also the finer moral intelligence, belonged to Ariel, rather than Prospero.

In the winter of 1998, Adrian Noble directed the play for the RSC at Stratford-upon-Avon on a simple set of a circle of small rocks. Billowing layers of translucent fabric, variously lit, determined the location and atmosphere. Noble's *Tempest* seemed self-consciously to resist the postcolonial interpretations of so many recent productions, as Ferdinand, not Caliban or Ariel, was played by a black actor (Evroy Deer), so the multiracial casting had no obvious political point. This *Tempest* was mainly about Prospero's troubled mind: his anger and the uncertain and hard-won path to forgiveness. David Calder was a moody and volatile Duke, who, educated by both Miranda (Penny Laden) and Ariel (Scott Handy), slowly and movingly came to understand that "the rarer action is / In virtue" rather than in "vengeance" (5.1.27–28). In 1999, at the West Yorkshire Playhouse in Leeds, Ian McKellen played Prospero in Jude Kelley's production, which was set not in anything like Noble's luminous island, but in a grim prison cell, with chains and chalk marks indicating the weeks, months, and years of Prospero's stay. McKellen, dressed in ragged trousers reaching only to his pale calves and a moth-eaten sweater, played a world-weary Prospero, more than a little addled and all too happy to renounce his power at the end.

London's Globe Theatre offered two notable productions of *The Tempest*. First in 2000, Lenka Udovicki directed the play with Vanessa Redgrave provocatively cast as Prospero, here surprisingly restrained, an all-too-human duke, obviously uncomfortable with and uncertain of his power. Ariel (Geraldine Alexander), white-faced, white-haired, in white suit, impassively performed Prospero's bidding with neither pleasure nor resignation, during the storm scene dispassionately folding a paper boat that resulted in the sailors and nobles being tossed in the rigging. When Prospero finally freed her, he removed her suit, revealing a pink sheath beneath, and the now unconfined but vulnerable Ariel slid off the stage and made her way through the audience standing in the pit. It was, however, Jasper Britton's Caliban, repulsively covered with mud, sores, and barnacles, who dominated the production, mimicking Prospero, engaging the groundlings at the Globe (even one night ad-libbing to their overactive involvement: "Look, I do the gags; okay?"). Even Prospero finally bowed to his charms, at the end handing him his fedora. Caliban put it on, fixed it carefully on his head, stood up straight, and exited to cheers. In the summer of 2005, Mark Rylance's last as the Globe's artistic director, Tim Carroll directed a three-person *Tempest*. Rylance, Alex Hassell, and Edward Hogg performed all the roles in a production that demanded as much concentration from the audience as from the actors. Sometimes confused and often confusing, the production at its best revealed unexpected aspects of the play, the multiple roles exposing parallels in the plot not often recognized in performance. The production took its inspiration from psychologist Noel Cobb's *Prospero's Island*, which views *The Tempest* as a Jungian allegory. At the reconstructed Globe, Ariel and Caliban became the opposed sides of Prospero's nature, with the play itself as a projection of Prospero's mind, an externalization of Prospero's internal psychodrama. If this did not always succeed, it reminded us again of the theatrical richness of this remarkable play that always points us toward the magic of Shakespeare's own art.

THE TEMPEST
ON SCREEN

Shakespeare could not, of course, have imagined a world in which people would see performances of his plays projected onto large or small screens rather than acted live in theaters, but that has become the case. In the more than one hundred years since the first film of a Shakespeare play was made (in 1899, an excerpt from Sir Herbert Beerbohm Tree's production of *King John*), the screen has become Shakespeare's proper medium no less than the stage or the printed page. If Shakespeare's works are undisputedly literary classics and staples of our theatrical repertories, they have also inescapably become a part of the modern age's love affair with film. In a movie theater, on a television screen, or on a DVD player, Shakespeare's plays live for us, and thereby reach audiences much greater than those that fill our theaters.

It is, however, a development not always welcomed. Some critics complain that Shakespeare on screen is different from (and worse than) Shakespeare in the theater. Certainly it is a distinct experience to see a play in a darkened movie theater with actors larger than life. It is different, too, to see it on a television screen with actors smaller than they are in life, and where the experience of play watching is inevitably more private than in any theater.

But there are obvious advantages as well. On screen, performances are preserved and allowed easily to circulate. If films of Shakespeare may sometimes lack the exhilarating provisionality of live theater, they gain the not insignificant benefit of easy accessibility. In a town without a theater company one can see a Shakespeare play virtually at will. Some newly filmed version of a Shakespeare play is seemingly released every year. A video or

DVD can be rented even if the film itself has passed from the local cineplex. And on video we can replay—even interrupt—the performance, allowing it to repeat itself as we attend to details that might otherwise be missed.

Filmed Shakespeare is indeed different from staged Shakespeare or Shakespeare read, but it is no less valuable for being so. It provides a way—and for most of us the most convenient way—to see the plays. For people who cannot get to the theater and who find the printed text difficult to imagine as a theatrical experience, filmed Shakespeare offers easy access to a performance. For students for whom the language of a play often seems (and indeed is) stilted and archaic, the enactment clarifies the psychological and social relations of the characters. For all of us who love Shakespeare, his availability on film gives us an archive of performances to be viewed and enjoyed again and again. It is no less an authentic experience than seeing Shakespeare in the theater, for the modern theater (even the self-conscious anachronisms like the rebuilt Globe) imposes its own anachronisms upon the plays (as indeed does a modern printed edition like this one). And arguably, as many like to claim, if Shakespeare lived today he would most likely have left Stratford for Hollywood.

If one were to judge Shakespeare's *The Tempest* by its film offshoots alone, one might conclude that it is a pretty far-out play. Derek Jarman's 1979 version illustrates how this play has lent itself to experimental postmodernist approaches. Jarman cuts and rearranges to avoid the potential tedium of long dialogues and to reinforce the impression of several actions occurring at the same time. The opening storm scene, shot like other outdoor sequences with blue filters to create an illusory mood, turns out to be a product of Prospero's brooding, dreamlike imagination as he tosses and turns in bed. This Prospero (Heathcote Williams) is strikingly young, with a full shock of curly hair and the mien of a Romantic poet, caught up as Renaissance mage in the study of astrological diagrams and cabalistic symbols. Being a reclusive and mad devotee of the occult, he dwells in a medieval fortress (Stoneleigh Castle in Warwickshire) of winding staircases and

high-ceilinged gloomy interiors where shadowy figures are only
dimly perceptible by firelight or candlelight. Ariel (Karl
Johnson), dressed in a white boiler suit, shoes, and gloves, is dis-
engaged and pallid as Prospero's technical assistant; between
master and servant the relationship is sexually ambiguous and
subject to oscillations in the balance of power. To Jarman, Ariel
is "a projection of Prospero's mind" struggling "to free itself and
escape." Miranda (Toyah Willcox) is very unlike her father:
adolescent, inventive, adventurous, gleefully independent, on the
brink of young womanhood, and hence very aware of her body.
Jarman has described her as a nymphomaniac. She adorns her
hair with wisps of thread and tries on garments that hint at her
awakening interest in sexual union. Discovering the shipwrecked
Ferdinand (David Meyer) naked and asleep on a pile of straw in
Caliban's lair, she is pitying and distressed when her father angrily
manacles the young man and obliges him to put on a white uni-
form. Caliban, played by Jack Birkett, also known as "the
Incredible Orlando," is hulking, bald, ungainly, and outfitted with
terrible teeth. He shambles, grimaces, drools, whines, makes fart-
ing noises, and leers voyeuristically at Miranda, who seems unfazed
by these attentions. He has a passion for raw eggs. In a flashback
we see this huge man as a baby, nuzzling at the breast of his
grotesquely naked mother, Sycorax, while a tied-up Ariel looks
on. Caliban's North Country accent and black skin invite us to
ponder troubled issues of racial, colonial, and regional conflict.

This is a deliberately transgressive *Tempest*, suffused with
the ideological animus of a director who links social compla-
cency and capitalist philistinism with homophobia and racial
prejudice, and who is fully ready to discover sadomasochistic
fantasies in Prospero's aggressive treatment of Ferdinand and
Caliban. Homoerotic resonances are juxtaposed against the insistent heterosexuality of Ferdinand and Miranda. Prospero's
masque, in Jarman's vision, becomes a bravura finale, with a
dance chorus of white-suited sailors accompanying the African
American blues singer Elisabeth Welsh as a combined Juno-
Ceres-Iris singing "Stormy Weather." Stephano and Trinculo
(Christopher Biggins and Peter Turner) are campy, giggly youths

doing funny walks and dancing drunkenly on the beach; Trinculo as drag queen elicits admiring wolf whistles from the handsome young sailors. Many reviewers and spectators have found this counterculture film offensive in its breaching of conventional social norms, but the transgressiveness is of course intentional, and Jarman's *Tempest* has received a good share of serious critical appraisal.

Peter Greenaway's *Prospero's Books* (1991) is no less avowedly revisionary and apocalyptic. Beginning with his concept of the play as a product of Prospero's imagination, Greenaway assigns all the speeches until the film's last moments to Prospero; John Gielgud's voice is heard throughout as the "author" of the story, high-voiced for Miranda and Ariel, more guttural and angry for Caliban, while on screen we behold actors (generally in Elizabethan costume, as contrasted with the nakedness of the islanders) acting out the meeting of the young lovers or the tribulations of the Italian party. The images are arresting in their visual singularity. Caliban (British dancer Michael Clark) emerges from a dark green grotto, lithe, slithery, reptilelike. His movements are mannered, choreographed, supple. In the arcaded, mysterious interior space that is more a site of cinematic imagination than a magician's cell, ranks of naked bodies, male and female, move rhythmically as the camera passes among them. They have no particular function in the story; instead, they are the human furniture of a cinematic dream. Prospero is furnished with twenty-four books, for which this film is named; as the story moves from the opening storm to other matters, the pages of these books come sequentially to life in *The Book of Water* (accompanied by a ship model appropriate to the storm), *A Book of Mirrors* (with mirror images of the infant Miranda tended to by ladies in waiting), *A Book of Mythologies* (giving background on the history of Prospero in Italy), *A Harsh Book of Geometry*, *The Vesalius Anatomy of Birth* (featuring a cutaway image of a woman's womb), *The Ninety-Two Concepts of the Minotaur*, *The Bath-house*, *The Book of Languages*, *The Book of Games* (the chess match of Ferdinand and Miranda), and finally *Thirty-Six Plays*, the 1623 Folio edition of Shakespeare's collected plays. This last has nineteen blank pages into which Prospero is to insert *The Tempest* once he has finished writing it.

Greenaway, himself a painter as well as a film director, borrows freely from Italian Renaissance painters and sculptors such as Bernini, Vesalius, Veronese, Bellini, da Vinci, Bronzini, and Botticelli for visual inspiration. He is insistent that the film's images should not be a simple substitution or restatement of Shakespeare's words, but should enjoy a life of their own. This film is a demonstration of how, in Greenaway's opinion as avant-garde artist, film should be self-reflexive, nonlinear, multiple in perspective, and multiple in its cross-fertilizing use of media, juxtaposing the visual and graphic arts with ballet and other forms of dance, music, and song as a way of evoking the mythological, anthropological, and psychological dimensions of Shakespeare's play. As with Jarman's film, this one by Greenaway has made many reviewers and audiences impatient with its self-indulgently repetitive sequences, but it has also won the respect of film critics for its visual inventiveness, its frame-within-frame techniques, its fascination with mirroring, and its psychological struggle to come to terms with female sexuality; even the insistent repetitions can be seen as deliberate unfoldings in what Mariacristina Cavecchi calls an "esthetic of redundancy."

Other versions extend the range of orthodoxy and unorthodoxy in the filming of this play. A 1905 two-minute silent-film selection records the opening storm scene in Herbert Beerbohm Tree's long-running production at His Majesty's Theatre in London. Peggy Ashcroft played Miranda in a ninety-minute BBC production in 1939, filmed on an austere budget. The *Hallmark Hall of Fame* ninety-minute *Tempest* on NBC in 1960, designed and directed by George Schaefer, starred Maurice Evans as Prospero, Lee Remick as Miranda, Roddy McDowell as Ariel, and Richard Burton as Caliban. Peter Brook released a twenty-seven-minute documentary version in France in 1968, demonstrating some remarkable filming techniques that focused on ship models for the storm with actors perched above the commotion on a trapeze. Cedric Messina produced *The Tempest* for the BBC's Play of the Month, also in 1968, with a strong cast that included Michael Redgrave as Prospero, Keith Mitchell as Caliban, and Jack MacGowran as Trinculo. For the BBC series of the Shakespeare plays, director John Gorrie in 1979 based his island of *The Tempest* on Gustave Doré's illustrations for Dante's *Divine Comedy*; with Michael Hordern as Prospero, Derek Godfrey as Antonio, Nigel Hawthorne as Stephano, and Pippa and Christopher Guard as sulky teenagers in the persons of Miranda and Ferdinand, this show is strongly cast but mundane in direction and without much comedy.

Not surprisingly, a play that has given occasion to such controversial and avant-garde productions as those of Jarman and Greenaway has also inspired some freewheeling adaptations. *Forbidden Planet* (1956) translates the play into a spaceship odyssey to Planet Altair IV, where Dr. Morbius (Walter Pidgeon) is marooned with his daughter Altaira (Anne Francis) and with Robby the Robot, a Michelin-man-resembling forebear of C-3PO and Robocop, in the role of Ariel. A spaceship under the command of J. J. Adams (Leslie Nielsen), looking for survivors, makes a landing on the planet and must then cope with the Id monster, a distant equivalent of Caliban. James Mason and Helen Mirren are Prospero and Miranda in *Age of Consent*, a 1970 film about a painter in self-imposed exile on a small island off Australia. Paul Mazursky's 1982 *Tempest* updates the play to twentieth-century New York, where an architect named Philip Dimitrious (John Cassavetes), dismayed at the adulterous liaison of his wife, Antonia (Gena Rowlands), with real estate tycoon Alonzo (Vittorio Gassman), flees with his teenage daughter, Miranda (Molly Ringwald), to a Greek island and takes up with a twice-divorced American cabaret singer named Aretha (Susan Sarandon), who fleetingly occupies the role of the play's Ariel. Among the island's other occupants are a randy goatherd, Kalibanos (Raul Julia), who makes every attempt to deflower Miranda; Alonzo's son Freddy (played by Sam Robards as the Ferdinand of this story); and Trinc (i.e., Trinculo), played as a stand-up comedian by Jackie Gayle. Some of the song and dance sequences are engaging and *Tempest*-like. Earlier, in 1979, a different sort of takeoff from *The Tempest* is to be found in *The Stuff of Dreams*, a prize-winning documentary about a 1960s hippie Vermont commune whose members undertake to produce the play as a utopian group project with gratifyingly cohering results. Jack Bender's 1998–99 film updates the story (but not the language) of *The Tempest* to pre–Civil War Mississippi, with Peter Fonda as Gideon Prosper, who is so preoccupied with voodoo magic that he fails to attend to his plantation and is forced to start a new life in a Mississippi bayou with his daughter (Katherine Heigl).

The Tempest
Filmography

1. 1905 (storm scene from Sir Herbert Beerbohm Tree's stage production, 2 minutes)
   Charles Urban, director

   Antonio—Lyn Harding
   Ferdinand—Basil Gill
   Alonzo—S. A. Cookson
   Gonzalo—J. Fisher White
   Boatswain—W. A. Haines

2. 1908 (12 minutes)
   Clarendon Film Company
   Percy Stow, director

3. 1911 (10 minutes)
   Thanhouser Film Corporation
   Edwin Thanhouser, producer
   Edwin Thanhouser, director

   Miranda—Florence LaBadie
   Ferdinand—Ed Genung

4. 1939
   BBC
   Dallas Bower, producer
   Dallas Bower, director

   Prospero—John Abbott
   Miranda—Peggy Ashcroft
   Ariel—Stephen Haggard
   Caliban—George Devine

5. 1956—*Forbidden Planet*
   Metro-Goldwyn-Mayer
   Nicholas Nayfack, producer
   Fred McLeod Wilcox, director

   Dr. Morbius—Walter Pidgeon
   Altaira Morbius—Anne Francis
   Commander Adams—Leslie Nielsen

6. 1956
   BBC
   Ian Atkins and Robert Atkins, producers
   Ian Atkins and Robert Atkins, directors

   Prospero—Robert Eddison
   Miranda—Anna Barry
   Ariel—Patti Brooks
   Caliban—Robert Atkins

7. 1960
   Hallmark Hall of Fame
   George Schaefer, producer
   George Schaefer, director

   Prospero—Maurice Evans
   Miranda—Lee Remick

Ariel—Roddy McDowall
Caliban—Richard Burton

8. 1968
BBC
Cedric Messina, producer
Basil Coleman, director

Prospero—Michael Redgrave
Miranda—Tessa Wyatt
Ariel—Ronald Pickup
Caliban—Keith Michell

9. 1979
BBC/Time-Life Television
Cedric Messina, producer
John Gorrie, director

Prospero—Michael Hordern
Miranda—Pippa Guard
Ariel—David Dixon
Caliban—Warren Clarke
Ferdinand—Christopher Guard
Stephano—Nigel Hawthorne

10. 1979—*The Stuff of Dreams* (documentary including excerpts from *The Tempest*)
Monteverdi Films
John Carroll, Alan Dater, Susan Dater, and John Scagliotti, producers
John Carroll and John Scagliotti, directors

Prospero—John Carroll
Miranda—Sharon O'Sullivan
Ariel—Christopher Coutant
Caliban—Peter Gould
Gonzalo—Shoshana Rihn

11. 1980
    Boyd's Company
    Don Boyd, Sarah Radclyffe, Guy Ford, and
    Mordecai Schreiber, producers
    Derek Jarman, director

    Prospero—Heathcote Williams
    Miranda—Toyah Willcox
    Ariel—Karl Johnson
    Caliban—Jack Birkett

12. 1980
    Berkeley Shakespeare Festival
    Audrey E. Stanley, director

    Prospero—Julian López-Morilas
    Ariel—Jane Macfie
    Caliban—Peter Fitzsimmons

13. 1982 (adaptation, set in the twentieth century)
    Columbia Pictures
    Paul Mazursky, Steven Bernhardt, and
    Pato Guzman, producers
    Paul Mazursky and Irby Smith, directors

    Phillip—John Cassavetes
    Miranda—Molly Ringwald
    Aretha—Susan Sarandon
    Kalibanos—Raul Julia
    Antonia—Gena Rowlands

14. 1985
    Bard Productions
    Ken Campbell, producer
    William Woodman, director

Prospero—Efrem Zimbalist, Jr.
Miranda—J. E. Taylor
Ariel—Duane Black
Caliban—William Hootkins

15. 1991—*Prospero's Books*
    Kees Kasander, producer
    Peter Greenaway, director

    Prospero—John Gielgud
    Miranda—Isabelle Pasco
    Caliban—Michael Clark
    Ferdinand—Mark Rylance

16. 1992—*Shakespeare: The Animated Tales*
    BBC Wales/Soyuzmultfilm
    Dave Edwards, Elizabeth Babakhina, and
    Christopher Grace, producers
    Stanislav Sokolov, director
    Leon Garfield, adaptor

    Prospero—Timothy West
    Miranda—Katy Behean
    Ariel—Ella Hood
    Caliban—Alun Armstrong
    Narrator—Martin Jarvis

17. 1998 (adaptation, set during the American Civil War)
    Bonnie Raskin Productions
    Jack Bender, Bonnie Raskin, and James Bigwood,
    producers
    Jack Bender, director

    Gideon Prosper—Peter Fonda
    Miranda Prosper—Katherine Heigl
    Ariel—Harold Perrineau, Jr.
    Gator Man—John Pyper-Ferguson

THE PLAYHOUSE

From other contemporary evidence, including the stage directions and dialogue of Elizabethan plays, we can surmise that the various public theaters where Shakespeare's plays were produced (the Theatre, the Curtain, the Globe) resembled the Swan in many important particulars, though there must have been some variations as well. The public playhouses were essentially round, or polygonal, and open to the sky, forming an acting arena approximately 70 feet in diameter; they did not have a large curtain with which to open and close a scene, such as we see today in opera and some traditional theater. A platform measuring approximately 43 feet across and 27 feet deep, referred to in the de Witt drawing as the *proscaenium*, projected into the yard, *planities sive arena*. The roof, *tectum*, above the stage and supported by two pillars, could contain machinery for ascents and descents, as were required in several of Shakespeare's late plays. Above this roof was a hut, shown in the drawing with a flag flying atop it and a trumpeter at its door announcing the performance of a play. The underside of the stage roof, called the heavens, was usually richly decorated with symbolic figures of the sun, the moon, and the constellations. The platform stage stood at a height of 5½ feet or so above the yard, providing room under the stage for underworldly effects. A trapdoor, which is not visible in this drawing, gave access to the space below.

The structure at the back of the platform (labeled *mimorum aedes*), known as the tiring-house because it was the actors' attiring (dressing) space, featured at least two doors, as shown here. Some theaters seem to have also had a discovery space, or curtained recessed alcove, perhaps between the two doors—in which Falstaff could have hidden from the sheriff (*1 Henry IV*,

This early copy of a drawing by Johannes de Witt of the Swan Theatre in London (c. 1596), made by his friend Arend van Buchell, is the only surviving contemporary sketch of the interior of a public theater in the 1590s.

2.4) or Polonius could have eavesdropped on Hamlet and his mother (*Hamlet*, 3.4). This discovery space probably gave the actors a means of access to and from the tiring-house. Curtains may also have been hung in front of the stage doors on occasion. The de Witt drawing shows a gallery above the doors that extends across the back and evidently contains spectators. On occasions when action "above" demanded the use of this space, as when Juliet appears at her "window" (*Romeo and Juliet*, 2.2 and 3.5), the gallery seems to have been used by the actors, but large scenes there were impractical.

The three-tiered auditorium is perhaps best described by Thomas Platter, a visitor to London in 1599 who saw on that occasion Shakespeare's *Julius Caesar* performed at the Globe:

> The playhouses are so constructed that they play on a raised platform, so that everyone has a good view. There are different galleries and places [*orchestra, sedilia, porticus*], however, where the seating is better and more comfortable and therefore more expensive. For whoever cares to stand below only pays one English penny, but if he wishes to sit, he enters by another door [*ingressus*] and pays another penny, while if he desires to sit in the most comfortable seats, which are cushioned, where he not only sees everything well but can also be seen, then he pays yet another English penny at another door. And during the performance food and drink are carried round the audience, so that for what one cares to pay one may also have refreshment.

Scenery was not used, though the theater building itself was handsome enough to invoke a feeling of order and hierarchy that lent itself to the splendor and pageantry on stage. Portable properties, such as thrones, stools, tables, and beds, could be carried or thrust on as needed. In the scene pictured here by de Witt, a lady on a bench, attended perhaps by her waiting-gentlewoman, receives the address of a male figure. If Shakespeare had written *Twelfth Night* by 1596 for performance at the Swan, we could imagine Malvolio appearing like this as he bows before the Countess Olivia and her gentlewoman, Maria.

THE TEMPEST

Names of the Actors This list appears at the end of the play in the First Folio, in this order, with Miranda's name below that of the men, as was conventional in lists of the period.

3 **PROSPERO,** *the right* the rightful

9 **CALIBAN . . .** *slave* The Folio reads *"saluage,"* a common alternative spelling of *savage* but perhaps also with a resonance of being salvaged from shipwreck. *Slave* has a range of meanings: wretch, rascal, servile creature, one who is owned by another person, one who is divested of freedom and personal rights.

Names of the Actors

ALONSO, *King of Naples*

SEBASTIAN, *his brother*

PROSPERO, *the right Duke of Milan*

ANTONIO, *his brother, the usurping Duke of Milan*

FERDINAND, *son to the King of Naples*

GONZALO, *an honest old counselor*

ADRIAN *and*
FRANCISCO, } *lords*

CALIBAN, *a savage and deformed slave*

TRINCULO, *a jester*

STEPHANO, *a drunken butler*

MASTER *of a ship*

BOATSWAIN

MARINERS

MIRANDA, *daughter to Prospero*

ARIEL, *an airy spirit*

IRIS,
CERES,
JUNO, } *[presented by] spirits*
NYMPHS,
REAPERS,

[Other spirits attending on Prospero]

THE SCENE: *An uninhabited island*

1.1 *Location: On board ship, off the island's coast.*

3 **Good** i.e., It's good you've come, or, my good fellow
yarely nimbly

6 **Tend** Attend

7 **Blow** (Addressed to the wind.)

7–8 **if room enough** as long as we have sea room
enough.

10 **Play the men** Act like men, with spirit.

14 **Keep** Remain in

15 **good** good fellow

17 **roarers** waves or winds, or both; spoken to as though
they were "bullies" or "blusterers"

1.1 ᔐ *A tempestuous noise of thunder and lightning*
heard. Enter a Shipmaster and a Boatswain.

MASTER Boatswain!

BOATSWAIN Here, Master. What cheer?

MASTER Good, speak to th' mariners. Fall to't yarely, 3
or we run ourselves aground. Bestir, bestir!   *Exit.*

Enter Mariners.

BOATSWAIN Heigh, my hearts! Cheerly, cheerly, my
hearts! Yare, yare! Take in the topsail. Tend to th' Mas- 6
ter's whistle.—Blow till thou burst thy wind, if room 7
enough!   8

Enter Alonso, Sebastian, Antonio, Ferdinand,
Gonzalo, and others.

ALONSO Good Boatswain, have care. Where's the Master? Play the men.   10

BOATSWAIN I pray now, keep below.

ANTONIO Where is the Master, Boatswain?

BOATSWAIN Do you not hear him? You mar our labor.
Keep your cabins! You do assist the storm.   14

GONZALO Nay, good, be patient.   15

BOATSWAIN When the sea is. Hence! What cares these
roarers for the name of king? To cabin! Silence! Trou- 17
ble us not.

GONZALO Good, yet remember whom thou hast
aboard.

BOATSWAIN None that I more love than myself. You are
a councillor; if you can command these elements to

23 **work . . . present** bring calm to our present circumstances

24 **hand** handle

27 **hap** happen.

30–1 **complexion . . . gallows** appearance shows he was born to be hanged (and therefore, according to the proverb, in no danger of drowning).

33 **our . . . advantage** our own cable is of little benefit.

34 **case is miserable** circumstances are desperate.

36 **Bring . . . course** Sail her close to the wind by means of the mainsail.

38 **our office** i.e., the noise we make at our work.

39 **give o'er** give up

47 **warrant him for drowning** guarantee that he will never be drowned

49 **unstanched** insatiable, loose, unrestrained. (Suggesting also "incontinent" and "menstrual.")

50 **ahold** ahull, close to the wind.   **courses** sails; i.e., foresail as well as mainsail, set in attempt to get the ship back out into open water.

silence and work the peace of the present, we will not   23
hand a rope more. Use your authority. If you cannot,   24
give thanks you have lived so long and make yourself
ready in your cabin for the mischance of the hour, if it
so hap.—Cheerly, good hearts!—Out of our way,   27
I say.   *Exit.*

GONZALO I have great comfort from this fellow. Methinks he hath no drowning mark upon him; his com-   30
plexion is perfect gallows. Stand fast, good Fate, to his   31
hanging! Make the rope of his destiny our cable, for
our own doth little advantage. If he be not born to be   33
hanged, our case is miserable.   *Exeunt [courtiers].*   34

   Enter Boatswain.

BOATSWAIN Down with the topmast! Yare! Lower,
lower! Bring her to try wi'th' main course. (*A cry*   36
within.) A plague upon this howling! They are louder
than the weather or our office.   38

   Enter Sebastian, Antonio, and Gonzalo.

Yet again? What do you here? Shall we give o'er and   39
drown? Have you a mind to sink?

SEBASTIAN A pox o'your throat, you bawling, blasphe-
mous, incharitable dog!

BOATSWAIN Work you, then.

ANTONIO Hang, cur! Hang, you whoreson, insolent
noisemaker! We are less afraid to be drowned than
thou art.

GONZALO I'll warrant him for drowning, though the   47
ship were no stronger than a nutshell and as
leaky as an unstanched wench.   49

BOATSWAIN Lay her ahold, ahold! Set her two courses.   50
Off to sea again! Lay her off!

   Enter Mariners, wet.

53 **must . . . cold?** i.e., must we drown in the cold sea?

56 **merely** utterly

57 **wide-chapped** big-mouthed

57-8 **Would . . . tides!** (Pirates were hanged on the shore and left until three tides had come in.)

60 **at wid'st** wide open.　　**glut** swallow

61 **split** break apart.

66 **heath** heather.　　**furze** gorse, a weed growing on wasteland

67 **fain** rather

MARINERS   All lost! To prayers, to prayers! All lost!

       [*The Mariners run about in confusion, exiting at random.*]

BOATSWAIN   What, must our mouths be cold?   53

GONZALO

    The King and Prince at prayers! Let's assist them,

    For our case is as theirs.

SEBASTIAN   I am out of patience.

ANTONIO

    We are merely cheated of our lives by drunkards.   56

    This wide-chapped rascal! Would thou mightst lie

      drowning   57

    The washing of ten tides!

GONZALO   He'll be hanged yet,   58

    Though every drop of water swear against it

    And gape at wid'st to glut him.

    (*A confused noise within:*)   "Mercy on us!"—   60

    "We split, we split!"—"Farewell my wife and

      children!"—   61

    "Farewell, brother!"—"We split, we split, we split!"

                          [*Exit Boatswain.*]

ANTONIO   Let's all sink wi'th' King.

SEBASTIAN   Let's take leave of him.

                      Exit [*with Antonio*].

GONZALO   Now would I give a thousand furlongs of sea

    for an acre of barren ground: long heath, brown furze,   66

    anything. The wills above be done! But I would fain   67

    die a dry death.   *Exit.*

1.2 *Location: The island, near Prospero's cell.* (On the
   Elizabethan stage, this cell is implicitly at hand
   throughout the play, although in some scenes the
   convention of flexible distance allows us to imagine characters in other parts of the island.)

1 **art** magic

2 **allay** pacify

4 **welkin's cheek** sky's face

6 **brave** gallant, splendid

11 **or ere** before

13 **freighting souls** cargo of souls.   **collected** calm,
   composed.

14 **amazement** consternation.   **piteous** pitying

16 **but** except

19 **more better** of higher rank

20 **full** very

22 **meddle** mingle

1.2 〜 *Enter Prospero [in his magic cloak] and Miranda.*

MIRANDA
  If by your art, my dearest father, you have   1
  Put the wild waters in this roar, allay them.   2
  The sky, it seems, would pour down stinking pitch,
  But that the sea, mounting to th' welkin's cheek,   4
  Dashes the fire out. Oh, I have suffered
  With those that I saw suffer! A brave vessel,   6
  Who had, no doubt, some noble creature in her,
  Dashed all to pieces. Oh, the cry did knock
  Against my very heart! Poor souls, they perished.
  Had I been any god of power, I would
  Have sunk the sea within the earth or ere   11
  It should the good ship so have swallowed and
  The freighting souls within her.

PROSPERO   Be collected.   13
  No more amazement. Tell your piteous heart   14
  There's no harm done.

MIRANDA   Oh, woe the day!

PROSPERO   No harm.
  I have done nothing but in care of thee,   16
  Of thee, my dear one, thee, my daughter, who
  Art ignorant of what thou art, naught knowing
  Of whence I am, nor that I am more better   19
  Than Prospero, master of a full poor cell,   20
  And thy no greater father.

MIRANDA   More to know
  Did never meddle with my thoughts.

PROSPERO   'Tis time   22
  I should inform thee farther. Lend thy hand
  And pluck my magic garment from me. So,

           [laying down his magic cloak and staff]

26 **wreck** shipwreck

27 **virtue** essence

30 **perdition** loss

31 **Betid** happened

32 **Which** whom

35 **bootless inquisition** profitless inquiry

41 **Out** fully

45–6 **assurance . . . warrants** certainty that my memory
   guarantees.

50 **backward . . . time** abyss of the past.

Lie there, my art.—Wipe thou thine eyes. Have
  comfort.
The direful spectacle of the wreck, which touched   26
The very virtue of compassion in thee,   27
I have with such provision in mine art
So safely ordered that there is no soul—
No, not so much perdition as an hair   30
Betid to any creature in the vessel   31
Which thou heard'st cry, which thou saw'st sink. Sit
  down,   32
For thou must now know farther.

MIRANDA [*sitting*]   You have often
  Begun to tell me what I am, but stopped
  And left me to a bootless inquisition,   35
  Concluding, "Stay, not yet."

PROSPERO   The hour's now come;
  The very minute bids thee ope thine ear.
  Obey, and be attentive. Canst thou remember
  A time before we came unto this cell?
  I do not think thou canst, for then thou wast not
  Out three years old.

MIRANDA   Certainly, sir, I can.   41

PROSPERO
  By what? By any other house or person?
  Of anything the image, tell me, that
  Hath kept with thy remembrance.

MIRANDA   'Tis far off,
  And rather like a dream than an assurance   45
  That my remembrance warrants. Had I not   46
  Four or five women once that tended me?

PROSPERO
  Thou hadst, and more, Miranda. But how is it
  That this lives in thy mind? What see'st thou else
  In the dark backward and abysm of time?   50

51 **aught** anything

56 **piece** masterpiece, exemplar

59 **no worse issued** no less nobly born, descended.

63 **holp** helped

64 **teen . . . to** trouble I've caused you to remember or put
you to

65 **from** out of

68 **next** next to

70 **manage** management, administration

71 **seigniories** i.e., city-states of northern Italy

72 **prime** first in rank and importance

76 **to . . . stranger** i.e., withdrew from my responsibilities
as duke.   **transported** carried away

If thou rememb'rest aught ere thou cam'st here,   51
How thou cam'st here thou mayst.

MIRANDA   But that I do not.

PROSPERO
Twelve year since, Miranda, twelve year since,
Thy father was the Duke of Milan and
A prince of power.

MIRANDA   Sir, are not you my father?

PROSPERO
Thy mother was a piece of virtue, and   56
She said thou wast my daughter; and thy father
Was Duke of Milan, and his only heir
And princess no worse issued.

MIRANDA   Oh, the heavens!   59
What foul play had we, that we came from thence?
Or blessèd was't we did?

PROSPERO   Both, both, my girl.
By foul play, as thou say'st, were we heaved thence,
But blessedly holp hither.

MIRANDA   Oh, my heart bleeds   63
To think o'th' teen that I have turned you to,   64
Which is from my remembrance! Please you, farther.   65

PROSPERO
My brother and thy uncle, called Antonio—
I pray thee mark me—that a brother should
Be so perfidious!—he whom next thyself   68
Of all the world I loved, and to him put
The manage of my state, as at that time   70
Through all the seigniories it was the first,   71
And Prospero the prime duke, being so reputed   72
In dignity, and for the liberal arts
Without a parallel; those being all my study,
The government I cast upon my brother
And to my state grew stranger, being transported   76

79 **perfected** grown skillful

81 **trash** check a hound by tying a cord or weight to its
   neck. **overtopping** running too far ahead of the
   pack; surmounting, exceeding one's authority

81–3 **new . . . formed 'em** won the loyalty of my officers
   by appointing them to new posts, or replaced them
   with others who would be loyal to Antonio, or else re-
   defined the positions and their occupants

83–5 **having . . . ear** having now under his control both
   the officers and the positions, he set a tone for his rule
   according to his own inclination. (*Key* is also a
   metaphor for tuning stringed instruments.)

87 **verdure** vitality. **on't** of it.

90 **closeness** retirement, seclusion

91–2 **but . . . rate** i.e., were it not that its private nature
   caused me to neglect my public responsibilities, had a
   value far beyond what public opinion could appreciate,
   or, simply because it was done in such seclusion, had a
   value not appreciated by popular opinion

94 **good parent** (Alludes to the proverb that good parents
   often bear bad children; see also line 120.) **of** in

97 **sans** without. **lorded** raised to lordship, with
   power and wealth

99 **else** otherwise, additionally

100–2 **Who . . . lie** i.e., who, by repeatedly telling the lie
   (that he was indeed Duke of Milan), made his memory
   such a confirmed sinner against truth that he began to
   believe his own lie

103–5 **out . . . prerogative** as a result of his making himself my substitute and carrying out all the visible functions of royalty with all its rights and privileges.

And rapt in secret studies. Thy false uncle—
Dost thou attend me?

MIRANDA   Sir, most heedfully.

PROSPERO
Being once perfected how to grant suits,   79
How to deny them, who t'advance and who
To trash for overtopping, new created   81
The creatures that were mine, I say, or changed 'em,   82
Or else new formed 'em; having both the key   83
Of officer and office, set all hearts i'th' state   84
To what tune pleased his ear, that now he was   85
The ivy which had hid my princely trunk
And sucked my verdure out on't. Thou attend'st not.   87

MIRANDA
Oh, good sir, I do.

PROSPERO   I pray thee, mark me.
I, thus neglecting worldly ends, all dedicated
To closeness and the bettering of my mind   90
With that which, but by being so retired,   91
O'erprized all popular rate, in my false brother   92
Awaked an evil nature; and my trust,
Like a good parent, did beget of him   94
A falsehood in its contrary as great
As my trust was, which had indeed no limit,
A confidence sans bound. He being thus lorded   97
Not only with what my revenue yielded
But what my power might else exact, like one   99
Who, having into truth by telling of it,   100
Made such a sinner of his memory   101
To credit his own lie, he did believe   102
He was indeed the Duke, out o'th' substitution   103
And executing th'outward face of royalty   104
With all prerogative. Hence his ambition growing—   105
Dost thou hear?

MIRANDA   Your tale, sir, would cure deafness.

107–9 **To have . . . Milan** In order to eliminate all separation between his role and himself, he insisted on becoming the Duke of Milan in name as well as in fact.

110 **temporal royalties** practical prerogatives and responsibilities of a sovereign

111 **confederates** conspires, allies himself

112 **dry** thirsty.   **sway** power

113 **him** i.e., the King of Naples

114 **his . . . his** Antonio's . . . the King of Naples's.   **bend** make bow down

115 **yet** hitherto

117 **condition** pact.   **th'event** the outcome

119 **but** other than

122 **hearkens** listens to

123 **he** the King of Naples.   **in . . . premises** in return for the stipulation

125 **presently extirpate** at once remove

131 **ministers . . . purpose** agents employed to do this.   **thence** from there

134 **hint** prompting

PROSPERO

To have no screen between this part he played   107
And him he played it for, he needs will be   108
Absolute Milan. Me, poor man, my library   109
Was dukedom large enough. Of temporal royalties   110
He thinks me now incapable; confederates—   111
So dry he was for sway—wi'th' King of Naples   112
To give him annual tribute, do him homage,   113
Subject his coronet to his crown, and bend   114
The dukedom yet unbowed—alas, poor Milan!—   115
To most ignoble stooping.

MIRANDA   O the heavens!

PROSPERO

Mark his condition and th'event, then tell me   117
If this might be a brother.

MIRANDA   I should sin
To think but nobly of my grandmother.   119
Good wombs have borne bad sons.

PROSPERO   Now the condition.
This King of Naples, being an enemy
To me inveterate, hearkens my brother's suit,   122
Which was that he, in lieu o'th' premises   123
Of homage and I know not how much tribute,
Should presently extirpate me and mine   125
Out of the dukedom and confer fair Milan,
With all the honors, on my brother. Whereon,
A treacherous army levied, one midnight
Fated to th' purpose did Antonio open
The gates of Milan, and, i'th' dead of darkness,
The ministers for th' purpose hurried thence   131
Me and thy crying self.

MIRANDA   Alack, for pity!
I, not remembering how I cried out then,
Will cry it o'er again. It is a hint   134

135 **wrings** (1) constrains (2) wrings tears from

138 **impertinent** irrelevant.   **Wherefore** Why

139 **demanded** asked.   **wench** (Here a term of endearment.)

141–2 **set . . . bloody** i.e., make obvious their murderous intent. (From the practice of marking with the blood of the prey those who have participated in a successful hunt.)

143 **fairer** apparently more attractive

144 **few** few words.   **bark** ship

146 **butt** cask, tub

147 **Nor tackle** neither rigging

148 **quit** abandoned

151 **Did . . . wrong** i.e., pitied us even as they drove us on.

154 **Infusèd** filled, suffused

155 **decked** covered (with salt tears); adorned

156 **which** i.e., the smile

157 **undergoing stomach** courage to go on

That wrings mine eyes to 't.

PROSPERO   Hear a little further,   135
And then I'll bring thee to the present business
Which now's upon 's, without the which this story
Were most impertinent.

MIRANDA   Wherefore did they not   138
That hour destroy us?

PROSPERO   Well demanded, wench.   139
My tale provokes that question. Dear, they durst
    not,
So dear the love my people bore me, nor set   141
A mark so bloody on the business, but   142
With colors fairer painted their foul ends.   143
In few, they hurried us aboard a bark,   144
Bore us some leagues to sea, where they prepared
A rotten carcass of a butt, not rigged,   146
Nor tackle, sail, nor mast; the very rats   147
Instinctively have quit it. There they hoist us,   148
To cry to th' sea that roared to us, to sigh
To th' winds whose pity, sighing back again,
Did us but loving wrong.

MIRANDA   Alack, what trouble   151
Was I then to you!

PROSPERO   Oh, a cherubin
Thou wast that did preserve me. Thou didst smile,
Infusèd with a fortitude from heaven,   154
When I have decked the sea with drops full salt,   155
Under my burden groaned, which raised in me   156
An undergoing stomach, to bear up   157
Against what should ensue.

MIRANDA   How came we ashore?

PROSPERO   By Providence divine.
Some food we had, and some fresh water, that
A noble Neapolitan, Gonzalo,
Out of his charity, who being then appointed

165 **stuffs** supplies

166 **steaded much** been of much use.   **So, of** Similarly
out of

169 **Would** I wish

170 **But ever** i.e., someday

171 **sea sorrow** sorrowful adventure at sea.

173–4 **made . . . can** provided a more valuable education
than other royal children (of either sex) can enjoy

175 **vainer** more foolishly spent

180 **my dear lady** (Refers to Fortune, not Miranda.)

182 **zenith** height of fortune. (Astrological term.)

183 **influence** astrological power

184 **but omit** but ignore instead

186 **dullness** drowsiness

187 **give it way** let it happen (i.e., don't fight it).

188 **Come away** Come

Master of this design, did give us, with
Rich garments, linens, stuffs, and necessaries,   165
Which since have steaded much. So, of his
    gentleness,   166
Knowing I loved my books, he furnished me
From mine own library with volumes that
I prize above my dukedom.

MIRANDA   Would I might   169
But ever see that man!

PROSPERO   Now I arise.   170
                [*He puts on his magic cloak.*]
Sit still, and hear the last of our sea sorrow.   171
Here in this island we arrived; and here
Have I, thy schoolmaster, made thee more profit   173
Than other princes can, that have more time   174
For vainer hours and tutors not so careful.   175

MIRANDA
Heavens thank you for't! And now, I pray you, sir—
For still 'tis beating in my mind—your reason
For raising this sea storm?

PROSPERO   Know thus far forth:
By accident most strange, bountiful Fortune,
Now my dear lady, hath mine enemies   180
Brought to this shore; and by my prescience
I find my zenith doth depend upon   182
A most auspicious star, whose influence   183
If now I court not, but omit, my fortunes   184
Will ever after droop. Here cease more questions.
Thou art inclined to sleep. 'Tis a good dullness,   186
And give it way. I know thou canst not choose.   187
                [*Miranda sleeps.*]
Come away, servant, come! I am ready now.   188
Approach, my Ariel, come.

    Enter Ariel.

193 **task** make demands upon

194 **quality** (1) fellow spirits (2) abilities.

195 **to point** to the smallest detail

197 **beak** prow

198 **waist** midships.   **deck** poop deck at the stern

199 **flamed amazement** struck terror in the guise of fire, i.e., Saint Elmo's fire.

201 **distinctly** in different places

204 **sight-outrunning** swifter than sight.   **were not** could not have been.

205 **Neptune** Roman god of the sea

207 **trident** three-pronged weapon

208 **coil** tumult

210 **of the mad** such as madmen feel

214 **up-staring** standing on end

ARIEL
    All hail, great master, grave sir, hail! I come
    To answer thy best pleasure; be't to fly,
    To swim, to dive into the fire, to ride
    On the curled clouds, to thy strong bidding task   193
    Ariel and all his quality.

PROSPERO   Hast thou, spirit,   194
    Performed to point the tempest that I bade thee?   195

ARIEL   To every article.
    I boarded the King's ship. Now on the beak,   197
    Now in the waist, the deck, in every cabin,   198
    I flamed amazement. Sometime I'd divide   199
    And burn in many places; on the topmast,
    The yards, and bowsprit would I flame distinctly,   201
    Then meet and join. Jove's lightning, the precursors
    O'th' dreadful thunderclaps, more momentary
    And sight-outrunning were not. The fire and cracks   204
    Of sulfurous roaring the most mighty Neptune   205
    Seem to besiege and make his bold waves tremble,
    Yea, his dread trident shake.

PROSPERO   My brave spirit!   207
    Who was so firm, so constant, that this coil   208
    Would not infect his reason?

ARIEL   Not a soul
    But felt a fever of the mad and played   210
    Some tricks of desperation. All but mariners
    Plunged in the foaming brine and quit the vessel,
    Then all afire with me. The King's son, Ferdinand,
    With hair up-staring—then like reeds, not hair—   214
    Was the first man that leapt; cried, "Hell is empty
    And all the devils are here!"

PROSPERO   Why, that's my spirit!
    But was not this nigh shore?

ARIEL   Close by, my master.

219 **sustaining** protecting

220 **bad'st** ordered

221 **troops** groups

223 **cooling of** cooling

224 **angle** corner

225 **sad knot** (Folded arms are indicative of melancholy.)

228 **nook** bay

229 **dew** (Collected at midnight for magical purposes;
    compare with line 324.)

230 **still-vexed Bermudas** ever stormy Bermudas.
    (Perhaps refers to the then recent Bermuda shipwreck;
    see play Introduction. The Folio text reads
    "Bermoothes.")

232 **with . . . labor** by means of a spell added to all the la-
    bor they have undergone

235 **float** sea

240 **mid season** noon.

241 **glasses** hourglasses.

243 **pains** labors

PROSPERO
    But are they, Ariel, safe?

ARIEL   Not a hair perished.
    On their sustaining garments not a blemish,   219
    But fresher than before; and, as thou bad'st me,   220
    In troops I have dispersed them 'bout the isle.   221
    The King's son have I landed by himself,
    Whom I left cooling of the air with sighs   223
    In an odd angle of the isle, and sitting,   224
    His arms in this sad knot.   [He folds his arms.]

PROSPERO   Of the King's ship,   225
    The mariners, say how thou hast disposed,
    And all the rest o'th' fleet.

ARIEL   Safely in harbor
    Is the King's ship; in the deep nook, where once   228
    Thou called'st me up at midnight to fetch dew   229
    From the still-vexed Bermudas, there she's hid;   230
    The mariners all under hatches stowed,
    Who, with a charm joined to their suffered labor,   232
    I have left asleep. And for the rest o'th' fleet,
    Which I dispersed, they all have met again
    And are upon the Mediterranean float   235
    Bound sadly home for Naples,
    Supposing that they saw the King's ship wrecked
    And his great person perish.

PROSPERO   Ariel, thy charge
    Exactly is performed. But there's more work.
    What is the time o'th' day?

ARIEL   Past the mid season.   240

PROSPERO
    At least two glasses. The time twixt six and now   241
    Must by us both be spent most preciously.

ARIEL
    Is there more toil? Since thou dost give me pains,   243

244 **remember** remind

251 **bate** remit, deduct

256 **do me** do for me.   **veins** veins of minerals, or, underground streams, thought to be analogous to the veins of the human body

257 **baked** hardened

259 **envy** malice

260 **grown into a hoop** i.e., so bent over with age as to resemble a hoop.

263 **Argier** Algiers

Let me remember thee what thou hast promised,   244
Which is not yet performed me.

PROSPERO   How now? Moody?
What is't thou canst demand?

ARIEL   My liberty.

PROSPERO
Before the time be out? No more!

ARIEL   I prithee,
Remember I have done thee worthy service,
Told thee no lies, made thee no mistakings, served
Without or grudge or grumblings. Thou did promise
To bate me a full year.

PROSPERO   Dost thou forget   251
From what a torment I did free thee?

ARIEL   No.

PROSPERO
Thou dost, and think'st it much to tread the ooze
Of the salt deep,
To run upon the sharp wind of the north,
To do me business in the veins o'th' earth   256
When it is baked with frost.

ARIEL   I do not, sir.   257

PROSPERO
Thou liest, malignant thing! Hast thou forgot
The foul witch Sycorax, who with age and envy   259
Was grown into a hoop? Hast thou forgot her?   260

ARIEL   No, sir.

PROSPERO
Thou hast. Where was she born? Speak. Tell me.

ARIEL
Sir, in Argier.

PROSPERO   Oh, was she so? I must   263
Once in a month recount what thou hast been,

268 **one . . . did** (Perhaps a reference to her pregnancy, for which her life would be spared.)

271 **blue-eyed** with dark circles under the eyes or with blue eyelids, implying pregnancy.   **with child** pregnant

274 **for** because

276 **hests** commands

283 **as mill wheels strike** as the blades of a mill wheel strike the water.

284 **Save** except.   **litter** give birth to

285 **whelp** offspring. (Used of animals.)   **hag-born** born of a female demon

286 **Yes . . . son** (Ariel is probably concurring with Prospero's comment about a "freckled whelp," not contradicting the point about "A human shape.")

287 **Dull . . . so** i.e., Exactly, that's what I said, you dullard

294 **gape** open wide

Which thou forget'st. This damned witch Sycorax,
For mischiefs manifold and sorceries terrible
To enter human hearing, from Argier,
Thou know'st, was banished. For one thing she did   268
They would not take her life. Is not this true?

ARIEL   Ay, sir.

PROSPERO
This blue-eyed hag was hither brought with child   271
And here was left by th' sailors. Thou, my slave,
As thou report'st thyself, was then her servant;
And, for thou wast a spirit too delicate   274
To act her earthy and abhorred commands,
Refusing her grand hests, she did confine thee,   276
By help of her more potent ministers
And in her most unmitigable rage,
Into a cloven pine, within which rift
Imprisoned thou didst painfully remain
A dozen years; within which space she died
And left thee there, where thou didst vent thy
    groans
As fast as mill wheels strike. Then was this island—   283
Save for the son that she did litter here,   284
A freckled whelp, hag-born—not honored with   285
A human shape.

ARIEL   Yes, Caliban her son.   286

PROSPERO
Dull thing, I say so: he, that Caliban   287
Whom now I keep in service. Thou best know'st
What torment I did find thee in. Thy groans
Did make wolves howl, and penetrate the breasts
Of ever-angry bears. It was a torment
To lay upon the damned, which Sycorax
Could not again undo. It was mine art,
When I arrived and heard thee, that made gape   294
The pine and let thee out.

297 **his** its
299 **correspondent** responsive, submissive
300 **spriting gently** duties as a spirit willingly.
310 **Heaviness** drowsiness
314 **miss** do without
315 **offices** functions, duties

ARIEL   I thank thee, master.

PROSPERO
If thou more murmur'st, I will rend an oak
And peg thee in his knotty entrails till   297
Thou hast howled away twelve winters.

ARIEL   Pardon, master.
I will be correspondent to command   299
And do my spriting gently.   300

PROSPERO   Do so, and after two days
I will discharge thee.

ARIEL   That's my noble master!
What shall I do? Say what? What shall I do?

PROSPERO
Go make thyself like a nymph o'th' sea. Be subject
To no sight but thine and mine, invisible
To every eyeball else. Go take this shape
And hither come in't. Go, hence with diligence!
                                        Exit [Ariel].
[*To Miranda*] Awake, dear heart, awake! Thou hast
    slept well.
Awake!

MIRANDA   The strangeness of your story put
Heaviness in me.

PROSPERO   Shake it off. Come on,   310
We'll visit Caliban, my slave, who never
Yields us kind answer.

MIRANDA   'Tis a villain, sir,
I do not love to look on.

PROSPERO   But, as 'tis,
We cannot miss him. He does make our fire,   314
Fetch in our wood, and serves in offices   315
That profit us.—What ho! Slave! Caliban!
Thou earth, thou! Speak.

CALIBAN (*within*)   There's wood enough within.

319 **When** (An exclamation of impatience.)

320 **quaint** ingenious

322 **got** begotten, sired

323 **dam** mother. (Used of animals.)

324 **wicked** mischievous, harmful

325 **fen** marsh, bog

326 **southwest** i.e., wind thought to bring disease

329 **Urchins** Hedgehogs; here, suggesting goblins in the guise of hedgehogs

330 **vast** lengthy, desolate time. (Malignant spirits were thought to be restricted to the hours of darkness.)

332 **as honeycomb** i.e., as a honeycomb full of bees

333 **'em** i.e., the honeycomb.

338 **the bigger . . . less** i.e., the sun and the moon. (See Genesis 1:16: "God then made two great lights: the greater light to rule the day, and the less light to rule the night.")

PROSPERO

Come forth, I say! There's other business for thee.

Come, thou tortoise! When?   319

Enter Ariel like a water nymph.

Fine apparition! My quaint Ariel,   320

Hark in thine ear.   [*He whispers.*]

ARIEL   My lord, it shall be done.   *Exit.*

PROSPERO

Thou poisonous slave, got by the devil himself   322

Upon thy wicked dam, come forth!   323

Enter Caliban.

CALIBAN

As wicked dew as e'er my mother brushed   324

With raven's feather from unwholesome fen   325

Drop on you both! A southwest blow on ye   326

And blister you all o'er!

PROSPERO

For this, be sure, tonight thou shalt have cramps,

Side-stitches that shall pen thy breath up. Urchins   329

Shall forth at vast of night that they may work   330

All exercise on thee. Thou shalt be pinched

As thick as honeycomb, each pinch more stinging   332

Than bees that made 'em.

CALIBAN   I must eat my dinner.   333

This island's mine, by Sycorax my mother,

Which thou tak'st from me. When thou cam'st first,

Thou strok'st me and made much of me, wouldst give
   me

Water with berries in't, and teach me how

To name the bigger light, and how the less,   338

That burn by day and night. And then I loved thee

And showed thee all the qualities o'th'isle,

The fresh springs, brine pits, barren place and fertile.

342 **charms** spells

345 **sty** confine as in a sty

348 **stripes** lashes

349 **humane** (Not distinguished as a word from *human*.)

353 **peopled else** otherwise populated

354–65 **Abhorrèd . . . prison** (Sometimes assigned by editors to Prospero.)

355 **print** imprint, impression

360 **purposes** meanings, desires

361 **race** natural disposition; species, nature

367 **red plague** plague characterized by red sores and evacuation of blood.   **rid** destroy

368 **learning** teaching.   **Hagseed** Offspring of a female demon

369 **thou'rt best** you'd be well advised

Cursed be I that did so! All the charms   342
Of Sycorax, toads, beetles, bats, light on you!
For I am all the subjects that you have,
Which first was mine own king; and here you sty me   345
In this hard rock, whiles you do keep from me
The rest o'th'island.

PROSPERO   Thou most lying slave,
  Whom stripes may move, not kindness! I have used
      thee,   348
  Filth as thou art, with humane care, and lodged thee   349
  In mine own cell, till thou didst seek to violate
  The honor of my child.

CALIBAN
  Oho, oho! Would't had been done!
  Thou didst prevent me; I had peopled else   353
  This isle with Calibans.

MIRANDA   Abhorrèd slave,   354
  Which any print of goodness wilt not take,   355
  Being capable of all ill! I pitied thee,
  Took pains to make thee speak, taught thee each hour
  One thing or other. When thou didst not, savage,
  Know thine own meaning, but wouldst gabble like
  A thing most brutish, I endowed thy purposes   360
  With words that made them known. But thy vile race,   361
  Though thou didst learn, had that in't which good
      natures
  Could not abide to be with; therefore wast thou
  Deservedly confined into this rock,
  Who hadst deserved more than a prison.   365

CALIBAN
  You taught me language, and my profit on't
  Is I know how to curse. The red plague rid you   367
  For learning me your language!

PROSPERO   Hagseed, hence!   368
  Fetch us in fuel, and be quick, thou'rt best,   369

370 **answer other business** perform other tasks.

372 **old** such as old people suffer, or, plenty of

373 **aches** (Pronounced "aitches.")

376 **Setebos** (A god of the Patagonians, named in Richard Eden's *History of Travel*, 1577.)

377.2 *Ariel, invisible* (Ariel wears a garment that by convention indicates he is invisible to Ferdinand and Miranda.)

380 **Curtsied . . . have** when you have curtsied

380–1 **kissed . . . whist** kissed the waves into silence, or, kissed while the waves are being hushed

382 **Foot it featly** dance nimbly

383 **sprites** spirits

384 **burden** refrain, undersong.

385 **s.d.** *dispersedly* i.e., from all directions, not in unison

392 **waits upon** serves, attends

393 **bank** sandbank

To answer other business. Shrugg'st thou, malice?   370
If thou neglect'st or dost unwillingly
What I command, I'll rack thee with old cramps,   372
Fill all thy bones with aches, make thee roar   373
That beasts shall tremble at thy din.

CALIBAN   No, pray thee.
  [*Aside*]   I must obey. His art is of such power
It would control my dam's god, Setebos,   376
And make a vassal of him.

PROSPERO   So, slave, hence!   377

                                    Exit Caliban.

        Enter Ferdinand; and Ariel, invisible, playing and
        singing. [Ferdinand does not see Prospero and
        Miranda.]

                    Ariel's Song.

ARIEL
        Come unto these yellow sands,
            And then take hands;
        Curtsied when you have, and kissed   380
            The wild waves whist;   381
        Foot it featly here and there,   382
            And, sweet sprites, bear   383
        The burden. Hark, hark!   384
                Burden, dispersedly [within]. Bow-wow. 385
        The watchdogs bark.
                    [*Burden, dispersedly within.*] Bow-wow.
        Hark, hark! I hear
        The strain of strutting chanticleer
            Cry Cock-a-diddle-dow.

FERDINAND
        Where should this music be? I'th'air or th'earth?
        It sounds no more; and sure it waits upon   392
        Some god o'th'island. Sitting on a bank,   393

396 **passion** grief
397 **Thence** i.e., From the bank on which I sat
406 **knell** announcement of a death by the tolling of a bell.
409 **remember** commemorate
411 **owes** owns.
412 **advance** raise
415 **brave** excellent
418 **but . . . stained** were it not that his luster is somewhat darkened
419 **canker** cankerworm (feeding on buds and leaves)

Weeping again the King my father's wreck,
This music crept by me upon the waters,
Allaying both their fury and my passion   396
With its sweet air. Thence I have followed it,   397
Or it hath drawn me rather. But 'tis gone.
No, it begins again.

                    Ariel's Song.

ARIEL
    Full fathom five thy father lies.
        Of his bones are coral made.
    Those are pearls that were his eyes.
        Nothing of him that doth fade
    But doth suffer a sea change
    Into something rich and strange.
    Sea nymphs hourly ring his knell.   406
                    Burden [*within*]. Ding dong.
    Hark, now I hear them, ding dong bell.

FERDINAND
    The ditty does remember my drowned father. 409
    This is no mortal business, nor no sound
    That the earth owes. I hear it now above me. 411

PROSPERO [*to Miranda*]
    The fringèd curtains of thine eye advance   412
    And say what thou see'st yond.

MIRANDA   What is't? A spirit?
    Lord, how it looks about! Believe me, sir,
    It carries a brave form. But 'tis a spirit. 415

PROSPERO
    No, wench, it eats and sleeps and hath such senses
    As we have, such. This gallant which thou see'st
    Was in the wreck; and, but he's something stained 418
    With grief, that's beauty's canker, thou mightst
        call him   419

426 **airs** songs.   **Vouchsafe** Grant

427 **remain** dwell

429 **bear me** conduct myself.   **prime** chief

430 **wonder** (Miranda's name means "to be wondered at.")

431 **maid** (1) a human maiden as opposed to a goddess (2) unmarried (3) a virgin

433 **best** i.e., in birth

436 **A single . . . now** (1) A single figure who combines into one person both self and King of Naples (since Ferdinand believes he has inherited the kingship) (2) A lonely shipwrecked figure

437 **Naples** the King of Naples.   **He . . . me** I who hear my own words am the King of Naples

438 **And . . . weep** i.e., and I weep at this reminder that my father is seemingly dead, leaving me heir.

439 **never . . . ebb** never dry, continually weeping

442 **son** (The only reference in the play to a son of Antonio.)

443 **more braver** more splendid.   **control** refute

A goodly person. He hath lost his fellows
And strays about to find 'em.

MIRANDA   I might call him
A thing divine, for nothing natural
I ever saw so noble.

PROSPERO [*aside*]   It goes on, I see,
As my soul prompts it.—Spirit, fine spirit, I'll free thee
Within two days for this.

FERDINAND [*seeing Miranda*] Most sure, the goddess
On whom these airs attend!—Vouchsafe my prayer   426
May know if you remain upon this island,   427
And that you will some good instruction give
How I may bear me here. My prime request,   429
Which I do last pronounce, is—O you wonder!—   430
If you be maid or no?

MIRANDA   No wonder, sir,   431
But certainly a maid.

FERDINAND   My language? Heavens!
I am the best of them that speak this speech,   433
Were I but where 'tis spoken.

PROSPERO [*coming forward*]   How? The best?
What wert thou if the King of Naples heard thee?

FERDINAND

A single thing, as I am now, that wonders   436
To hear thee speak of Naples. He does hear me,   437
And that he does I weep. Myself am Naples,   438
Who with mine eyes, never since at ebb, beheld   439
The King my father wrecked.

MIRANDA   Alack, for mercy!

FERDINAND

Yes, faith, and all his lords, the Duke of Milan
And his brave son being twain.

PROSPERO [*aside*]   The Duke of Milan   442
And his more braver daughter could control thee,   443

445 **changed eyes** exchanged amorous glances.

447 **done . . . wrong** i.e., spoken falsely.

454 **both in either's** each in the other's

455 **uneasy** difficult

456 **light** cheap. (Playing on *light,* "easy," in 455.)

457 **attend** follow, obey

458 **ow'st** ownest

460 **on't** of it.

463 **strive . . . with't** i.e., expel the evil and occupy the *temple,* the body.

If now 'twere fit to do't. At the first sight
They have changed eyes.—Delicate Ariel,   445
I'll set thee free for this. [*To Ferdinand*] A word, good
    sir.
I fear you have done yourself some wrong. A word!   447

MIRANDA [*aside*]
Why speaks my father so ungently? This
Is the third man that e'er I saw, the first
That e'er I sighed for. Pity move my father
To be inclined my way!

FERDINAND [*to Miranda*]   Oh, if a virgin,
And your affection not gone forth, I'll make you
The Queen of Naples.

PROSPERO   Soft, sir! One word more.
[*Aside*] They are both in either's powers; but this swift
    business   454
I must uneasy make, lest too light winning   455
Make the prize light. [*To Ferdinand*] One word more: I
    charge thee   456
That thou attend me. Thou dost here usurp   457
The name thou ow'st not, and hast put thyself   458
Upon this island as a spy, to win it
From me, the lord on't.

FERDINAND   No, as I am a man.   460

MIRANDA
There's nothing ill can dwell in such a temple.
If the ill spirit have so fair a house,
Good things will strive to dwell with't.

PROSPERO   Follow me.—   463
Speak not you for him; he's a traitor.—Come,
I'll manacle thy neck and feet together.
Seawater shalt thou drink; thy food shall be
The fresh-brook mussels, withered roots, and husks
Wherein the acorn cradled. Follow.

469 **entertainment** treatment

470 **s.d.** *charmed* magically prevented

471 **rash** harsh

472 **gentle** (1) wellborn (2) easily managed. **fearful** frightening, dangerous.

473 **My . . . tutor?** i.e., Do you, as my daughter and thus bound to me by obedience, dare presume to teach me what to do?

475 **ward** defensive posture (in fencing)

479 **surety** guarantee.

484 **To** compared with

488 **nerves** sinews

490 **spirits** vital powers

FERDINAND   No!
I will resist such entertainment till   469
Mine enemy has more pow'r.

          He draws, and is charmed from moving.

MIRANDA   O dear father,   470
Make not too rash a trial of him, for   471
He's gentle, and not fearful.

PROSPERO   What, I say,   472
My foot my tutor?—Put thy sword up, traitor,   473
Who mak'st a show but dar'st not strike, thy
     conscience
Is so possessed with guilt. Come, from thy ward,   475
For I can here disarm thee with this stick
And make thy weapon drop.   [*He brandishes his staff.*]

MIRANDA [*trying to hinder him*]   Beseech you, father!

PROSPERO
Hence! Hang not on my garments.

MIRANDA   Sir, have pity!
I'll be his surety.

PROSPERO   Silence! One word more   479
Shall make me chide thee, if not hate thee. What,
An advocate for an impostor? Hush!
Thou think'st there is no more such shapes as he,
Having seen but him and Caliban. Foolish wench,
To th' most of men this is a Caliban,   484
And they to him are angels.

MIRANDA   My affections
Are then most humble; I have no ambition
To see a goodlier man.

PROSPERO [*to Ferdinand*]   Come on, obey.
Thy nerves are in their infancy again   488
And have no vigor in them.

FERDINAND   So they are.
My spirits, as in a dream, are all bound up.   490

493 **light** unimportant

495 **corners else** other corners, regions

499 **me** for me.

501 **unwonted** unusual

503 **then** if so, then

2.1 *Location: Another part of the island.*

3 **hint** occasion

5 **The masters . . . the merchant** the officers or owners of some merchant vessel and the merchant who owns the cargo

6 **for** as for

My father's loss, the weakness which I feel,
The wreck of all my friends, nor this man's threats
To whom I am subdued, are but light to me,   493
Might I but through my prison once a day
Behold this maid. All corners else o'th'earth   495
Let liberty make use of; space enough
Have I in such a prison.

PROSPERO [aside]   It works. [To Ferdinand] Come on.—
Thou hast done well, fine Ariel! [To Ferdinand] Follow
    me.
[To Ariel] Hark what thou else shalt do me.

MIRANDA [to Ferdinand]   Be of comfort. 499
My father's of a better nature, sir,
Than he appears by speech. This is unwonted   501
Which now came from him.

PROSPERO [to Ariel]   Thou shalt be as free
As mountain winds; but then exactly do   503
All points of my command.

ARIEL   To th' syllable.

PROSPERO [to Ferdinand]
Come, follow. [To Miranda] Speak not for him.

                                        Exeunt.

2.1 ∽ *Enter Alonso, Sebastian, Antonio, Gonzalo,*
        Adrian, Francisco, and others.

GONZALO [to Alonso]
Beseech you, sir, be merry. You have cause,
So have we all, of joy, for our escape
Is much beyond our loss. Our hint of woe   3
Is common; every day some sailor's wife,
The masters of some merchant, and the merchant,   5
Have just our theme of woe. But for the miracle,   6
I mean our preservation, few in millions

8–9 **weigh . . . comfort** balance our sorrow against our comfort.

11 **porridge** (Punningly suggested by *peace,* i.e., "peas" or "pease," a common ingredient of porridge.)

12 **visitor** one bringing nourishment and comfort to the sick, as Gonzalo is doing

12–13 **give him o'er** abandon him

17 **Tell** Keep count.

18–19 **When . . . entertainer** When every sorrow that presents itself is accepted without resistance, there comes to the recipient

20 **dollar** widely circulated coin, the German thaler and the Spanish piece of eight. (Sebastian puns on *entertainer* in the sense of paid performer or innkeeper; to Gonzalo, *dollar* suggests "dolor," grief.)

27 **spare** forbear, cease.

30–1 **Which . . . crow?** Which of the two, Gonzalo or Adrian, do you bet will speak (crow) first?

32 **The old cock** Gonzalo.

33 **The cockerel** Adrian.

35 **laughter** (1) burst of laughter (2) sitting of eggs. (When Adrian, the *cockerel*, begins to speak two lines later, Sebastian loses the bet. The Folio speech prefixes in lines 38–9 are here reversed so that Antonio enjoys his laugh as the prize for winning, as in the proverb "He who laughs last laughs best" or "He laughs that wins." The Folio assignment can work in the theater, however, if Sebastian pays for losing with a sardonic laugh of concession.)

36 **A match!** A bargain; agreed!

37 **desert** uninhabited

Can speak like us. Then wisely, good sir, weigh   8
Our sorrow with our comfort.

ALONSO   Prithee, peace.   9

SEBASTIAN [*aside to Antonio*]   He receives comfort like
cold porridge.   11

ANTONIO [*aside to Sebastian*]   The visitor will not give   12
him o'er so.   13

SEBASTIAN   Look, he's winding up the watch of his wit;
by and by it will strike.

GONZALO [*to Alonso*]   Sir—

SEBASTIAN [*aside to Antonio*]   One. Tell.   17

GONZALO   When every grief is entertained   18
That's offered, comes to th' entertainer—   19

SEBASTIAN   A dollar.   20

GONZALO   Dolor comes to him, indeed. You have spoken truer than you purposed.

SEBASTIAN   You have taken it wiselier than I meant you
should.

GONZALO [*to Alonso*]   Therefore, my lord—

ANTONIO   Fie, what a spendthrift is he of his tongue!

ALONSO [*to Gonzalo*]   I prithee, spare.   27

GONZALO   Well, I have done. But yet—

SEBASTIAN [*aside to Antonio*]   He will be talking.

ANTONIO [*aside to Sebastian*]   Which, of he or Adrian,   30
for a good wager, first begins to crow?   31

SEBASTIAN   The old cock.   32

ANTONIO   The cockerel.   33

SEBASTIAN   Done. The wager?

ANTONIO   A laughter.   35

SEBASTIAN   A match!   36

ADRIAN   Though this island seem to be desert—   37

ANTONIO   Ha, ha, ha!

39 **you're paid** i.e., you've had your laugh.

43 **miss't** (1) avoid saying "Yet" (2) miss the island.

44 **must needs be** has to be

45 **temperance** mildness of climate.

46 **Temperance** a girl's name.   **delicate** (Here it means "given to pleasure, voluptuous"; in line 44, "pleasant." Antonio is evidently suggesting that *tender, and delicate temperance* sounds like a Puritan phrase, which Antonio then mocks by applying the words to a woman rather than an island. He began this bawdy comparison with a double entendre on *inaccessible*, line 40.)

47 **subtle** (Here it means "tricky, sexually crafty"; in line 44, "delicate.")

48 **delivered** uttered. (Sebastian joins Antonio in baiting the Puritans with his use of the pious cant phrase *learnedly delivered*.)

51 **fen** evil-smelling marshland.

53 **save** except

55 **lusty** healthy

57 **tawny** dull brown, yellowish.

58 **eye** tinge, or spot. (Sebastian is mocking Gonzalo's optimism by saying there's precious little green to see anywhere. Antonio echoes him in line 59 with similar sarcasm.)

60 **He . . . totally** i.e., He's only a tiny 100 percent wrong. (Sarcastic.)

63 **As . . . are** (More sarcasm: Just as many alleged strange sights are doubtful, including this one.)

68–70 **If . . . report** (More wisecracking: Gonzalo's mud-filled pockets would surely give the lie to his talk of clean fresh garments, thereby *pocketing up* or tabling the *report*.)

SEBASTIAN   So, you're paid.   39

ADRIAN   Uninhabitable and almost inaccessible—

SEBASTIAN   Yet—

ADRIAN   Yet—

ANTONIO   He could not miss't.   43

ADRIAN   It must needs be of subtle, tender, and delicate   44
temperance.   45

ANTONIO   Temperance was a delicate wench.   46

SEBASTIAN   Ay, and a subtle, as he most learnedly   47
delivered.   48

ADRIAN   The air breathes upon us here most sweetly.

SEBASTIAN   As if it had lungs, and rotten ones.

ANTONIO   Or as 'twere perfumed by a fen.   51

GONZALO   Here is everything advantageous to life.

ANTONIO   True, save means to live.   53

SEBASTIAN   Of that there's none, or little.

GONZALO   How lush and lusty the grass looks! How   55
green!

ANTONIO   The ground indeed is tawny.   57

SEBASTIAN   With an eye of green in't.   58

ANTONIO   He misses not much.

SEBASTIAN   No. He doth but mistake the truth totally.   60

GONZALO   But the rarity of it is—which is indeed
almost beyond credit—

SEBASTIAN   As many vouched rarities are.   63

GONZALO   That our garments, being, as they were,
drenched in the sea, hold notwithstanding their fresh-
ness and glosses, being rather new-dyed than stained
with salt water.

ANTONIO   If but one of his pockets could speak, would   68
it not say he lies?   69

SEBASTIAN   Ay, or very falsely pocket up his report.   70

77 **to** for

78 **widow Dido** Queen of Carthage, deserted by Aeneas.
(She was, in fact, a widow when Aeneas, a widower,
met her, but Antonio may be amused at Gonzalo's
prudish use of the term "widow" to describe a woman
deserted by her lover.)

82 **take** understand, respond to, interpret

84 **study of** think about

88 **miraculous harp** (Alludes to Amphion's harp, with
which he raised the walls of Thebes; Gonzalo has ex-
ceeded that deed by re-creating ancient Carthage—
wall and houses—mistakenly on the site of modern-day
Tunis. Some Renaissance commentators believed, like
Gonzalo, that the two sites were near each other.)

94 **kernels** seeds

96 **Ay** (Gonzalo may be reasserting his point about
Carthage, or he may be responding ironically to
Antonio, who, in turn, answers sarcastically.)

97 **in good time** (An expression of ironical acquiescence
or amazement, i.e., "sure, right away.")

101 **rarest** most remarkable, beautiful

GONZALO   Methinks our garments are now as fresh as
when we put them on first in Afric, at the marriage of
the King's fair daughter Claribel to the King of Tunis.

SEBASTIAN   'Twas a sweet marriage, and we prosper
well in our return.

ADRIAN   Tunis was never graced before with such a
paragon to their queen.   77

GONZALO   Not since widow Dido's time.   78

ANTONIO [aside to Sebastian]   Widow? A pox o' that!
How came that "widow" in? Widow Dido!

SEBASTIAN   What if he had said "widower Aeneas"
too? Good Lord, how you take it!   82

ADRIAN [to Gonzalo]   "Widow Dido" said you? You make
me study of that. She was of Carthage, not of Tunis.   84

GONZALO   This Tunis, sir, was Carthage.

ADRIAN   Carthage?

GONZALO   I assure you, Carthage.

ANTONIO   His word is more than the miraculous harp.   88

SEBASTIAN   He hath raised the wall, and houses too.

ANTONIO   What impossible matter will he make easy
next?

SEBASTIAN   I think he will carry this island home in his
pocket and give it his son for an apple.

ANTONIO   And, sowing the kernels of it in the sea,   94
bring forth more islands.

GONZALO   Ay.   96

ANTONIO   Why, in good time.   97

GONZALO [to Alonso]   Sir, we were talking that our garments seem now as fresh as when we were at Tunis at
the marriage of your daughter, who is now queen.

ANTONIO   And the rarest that e'er came there.   101

102 **Bate** Abate, except, leave out. (Sebastian says sardon-
ically, surely you should allow widow Dido to be an ex-
ception.)

104 **doublet** close-fitting jacket

105 **in a sort** in a way.

106 **sort** (Antonio plays on the idea of drawing lots and on
"fishing" for something to say.)

109 **The stomach . . . sense** my appetite for hearing
them.

110 **Married** given in marriage

111 **rate** estimation, opinion

116 **surges** waves

120 **oared** propelled as by an oar

121 **lusty** vigorous

122 **that . . . bowed** that projected out over its (*his*) surf-
eroded base, bending down toward the sea

123 **As** as if

126 **That** you who

127 **But . . . her** but would rather turn her loose (or, "lose
her")

128–9 **Where . . . on't** where at least she is not a constant
reproach in your eye, which has good reason to weep
sorrowfully for this unhappy development.

SEBASTIAN   Bate, I beseech you, widow Dido.   102

ANTONIO   Oh, widow Dido? Ay, widow Dido.

GONZALO   Is not, sir, my doublet as fresh as the first   104
day I wore it? I mean, in a sort.   105

ANTONIO   That "sort" was well fished for.   106

GONZALO   When I wore it at your daughter's marriage.

ALONSO
You cram these words into mine ears against
The stomach of my sense. Would I had never   109
Married my daughter there! For, coming thence,   110
My son is lost and, in my rate, she too,   111
Who is so far from Italy removed
I ne'er again shall see her. O thou mine heir
Of Naples and of Milan, what strange fish
Hath made his meal on thee?

FRANCISCO   Sir, he may live.
I saw him beat the surges under him   116
And ride upon their backs. He trod the water,
Whose enmity he flung aside, and breasted
The surge most swoll'n that met him. His bold head
'Bove the contentious waves he kept, and oared   120
Himself with his good arms in lusty stroke   121
To th' shore, that o'er his wave-worn basis bowed,   122
As stooping to relieve him. I not doubt   123
He came alive to land.

ALONSO   No, no, he's gone.

SEBASTIAN [to Alonso]
Sir, you may thank yourself for this great loss,
That would not bless our Europe with your daughter,   126
But rather loose her to an African,   127
Where she at least is banished from your eye,   128
Who hath cause to wet the grief on't.

ALONSO   Prithee, peace.   129

130 **importuned** urged, implored

131–3 **the fair . . . bow** Claribel herself was poised uncertainly, as in a balancing scale, between being unwilling to marry and yet wishing to obey her father.

135 **of . . . making** on account of this marriage and subsequent shipwreck

138 **dear'st** heaviest, most costly

141 **time** appropriate time

142 **plaster** (A medical application.)

143 **chirurgeonly** like a skilled surgeon. (Antonio mocks Gonzalo's medical analogy of a *plaster* applied curatively to a wound.)

145 **Fowl** (With a pun on *foul*, returning to the imagery of lines 30–5.)

146 **plantation** colonial settlement. (With subsequent wordplay on the literal meaning, "planting.")

147 **docks . . . mallows** (Weeds; the first was used as an antidote for nettle stings.)

149 **Scape** Escape.   **want** lack. (Sebastian jokes sarcastically that this hypothetical ruler would be saved from dissipation only by the barrenness of the island.)

150 **by contraries** by what is directly opposite to usual custom

151 **traffic** trade

SEBASTIAN
   You were kneeled to and importuned otherwise   130
   By all of us, and the fair soul herself   131
   Weighed between loathness and obedience at   132
   Which end o'th' beam should bow. We have lost your
      son,   133
   I fear, forever. Milan and Naples have
   More widows in them of this business' making   135
   Than we bring men to comfort them.
   The fault's your own.

ALONSO   So is the dear'st o'th' loss.   138

GONZALO   My lord Sebastian,
   The truth you speak doth lack some gentleness
   And time to speak it in. You rub the sore   141
   When you should bring the plaster.

SEBASTIAN   Very well.   142

ANTONIO   And most chirurgeonly.   143

GONZALO [to Alonso]
   It is foul weather in us all, good sir,
   When you are cloudy.

SEBASTIAN [to Antonio]   Fowl weather?

ANTONIO [to Sebastian]   Very foul.   145

GONZALO
   Had I plantation of this isle, my lord—   146

ANTONIO [to Sebastian]
   He'd sow't with nettle seed.

SEBASTIAN   Or docks, or mallows.   147

GONZALO
   And were the king on't, what would I do?

SEBASTIAN   Scape being drunk for want of wine.   149

GONZALO
   I'th' commonwealth I would by contraries   150
   Execute all things; for no kind of traffic   151

153 **Letters** learning

154 **use of service** custom of employing servants. **succession** holding of property by right of inheritance

155 **Bourn . . . tilth** boundaries, property limits, tillage of soil

156 **corn** grain

164 **pike** lance.   **engine** instrument of warfare

166 **it** its.   **foison** plenty

171 **the Golden Age** an age of prelapsarian abundance and peace; the first of four "ages" of human history, followed by silver, bronze, and lead.   **'Save** God save

175 **minister occasion** furnish opportunity (for laughter)

176 **sensible** sensitive.   **use** are accustomed

Would I admit; no name of magistrate;
Letters should not be known; riches, poverty,   153
And use of service, none; contract, succession,   154
Bourn, bound of land, tilth, vineyard, none;   155
No use of metal, corn, or wine, or oil;   156
No occupation; all men idle, all,
And women too, but innocent and pure;
No sovereignty—

SEBASTIAN   Yet he would be king on't.

ANTONIO   The latter end of his commonwealth forgets
the beginning.

GONZALO
All things in common nature should produce
Without sweat or endeavor. Treason, felony,
Sword, pike, knife, gun, or need of any engine   164
Would I not have; but nature should bring forth,
Of it own kind, all foison, all abundance,   166
To feed my innocent people.

SEBASTIAN   No marrying 'mong his subjects?

ANTONIO   None, man, all idle—whores and knaves.

GONZALO
I would with such perfection govern, sir,
T'excel the Golden Age.

SEBASTIAN   'Save His Majesty!   171

ANTONIO
Long live Gonzalo!

GONZALO   And—do you mark me, sir?

ALONSO
Prithee, no more. Thou dost talk nothing to me.

GONZALO   I do well believe Your Highness, and did it
to minister occasion to these gentlemen, who are of   175
such sensible and nimble lungs that they always use   176
to laugh at nothing.

182 **An** If.   **flat-long** with the flat of the sword, i.e., inef-
fectually.

183 **mettle** temperament, courage. (The sense of *metal*, in-
distinguishable as a form from *mettle,* continues the
metaphor of the sword. F reads "mettal.")

184 **sphere** orbit. (Literally, one of the concentric zones
occupied by planets in Ptolemaic astronomy.)

186 **a-batfowling** hunting birds at night with lantern and
bat, or "stick"; also, gulling a simpleton. (Gonzalo is the
simpleton, or fowl, and Sebastian will use the moon as
his lantern.)

188–9 **adventure . . . weakly** risk my reputation for discretion for so trivial a cause (by getting angry).

190 **heavy** sleepy.

191 **Go . . . us** i.e., Get ready for sleep and we'll do our part
by laughing.

193 **Would . . . thoughts** would shut off my melancholy
brooding when they (my eyes) close themselves in
sleep.

195 **Do . . . it** do not decline the invitation to drowsiness.

ANTONIO   'Twas you we laughed at.

GONZALO   Who in this kind of merry fooling am nothing to you; so you may continue, and laugh at nothing still.

ANTONIO   What a blow was there given!

SEBASTIAN   An it had not fallen flat-long.   182

GONZALO   You are gentlemen of brave mettle; you   183
would lift the moon out of her sphere if she would   184
continue in it five weeks without changing.

Enter Ariel [invisible] playing solemn music.

SEBASTIAN   We would so, and then go a-batfowling.   186

ANTONIO   Nay, good my lord, be not angry.

GONZALO   No, I warrant you, I will not adventure my   188
discretion so weakly. Will you laugh me asleep? For I   189
am very heavy.   190

ANTONIO   Go sleep, and hear us.   191

[*All sleep except Alonso, Sebastian, and Antonio.*]

ALONSO
What, all so soon asleep? I wish mine eyes
Would, with themselves, shut up my thoughts. I find   193
They are inclined to do so.

SEBASTIAN   Please you, sir,
Do not omit the heavy offer of it.   195
It seldom visits sorrow; when it doth,
It is a comforter.

ANTONIO   We two, my lord,
Will guard your person while you take your rest,
And watch your safety.

ALONSO   Thank you. Wondrous heavy.

[*Alonso sleeps. Exit Ariel.*]

SEBASTIAN
What a strange drowsiness possesses them!

204 **They . . . consent** The others all fell asleep simultaneously, as if by common agreement

208 **Th'occasion . . . thee** The opportunity of the moment calls upon you

212 **sleepy** dreamlike, fantastic

217 **wink'st** (you) shut your eyes

218 **distinctly** articulately

221 **if heed** if you heed

222 **Trebles thee o'er** makes you three times as great and
rich.   **standing water** water that neither ebbs nor
flows, at a standstill.

ANTONIO

It is the quality o'th' climate.

SEBASTIAN   Why

Doth it not then our eyelids sink? I find not

Myself disposed to sleep.

ANTONIO   Nor I. My spirits are nimble.

They fell together all, as by consent;   204

They dropped, as by a thunderstroke. What might,

Worthy Sebastian, oh, what might—? No more.

And yet methinks I see it in thy face

What thou shouldst be. Th'occasion speaks thee, and   208

My strong imagination sees a crown

Dropping upon thy head.

SEBASTIAN   What, art thou waking?

ANTONIO

Do you not hear me speak?

SEBASTIAN   I do, and surely

It is a sleepy language, and thou speak'st   212

Out of thy sleep. What is it thou didst say?

This is a strange repose, to be asleep

With eyes wide open—standing, speaking, moving—

And yet so fast asleep.

ANTONIO   Noble Sebastian,

Thou let'st thy fortune sleep—die, rather; wink'st   217

Whiles thou art waking.

SEBASTIAN   Thou dost snore distinctly;   218

There's meaning in thy snores.

ANTONIO

I am more serious than my custom. You

Must be so too if heed me, which to do   221

Trebles thee o'er.

SEBASTIAN   Well, I am standing water.   222

ANTONIO

I'll teach you how to flow.

223 **ebb** recede, decline

224 **Hereditary sloth** i.e., natural laziness and the position of younger brother, one who cannot inherit

225–6 **If . . . mock it!** If you only knew how much you secretly cherish ambition even while your words mock it!

226–7 **How . . . invest it!** How the more you speak flippantly of ambition, the more you, in effect, affirm it, clothing what you have stripped!

228 **the bottom** i.e., on which unadventurous men may go aground and miss the tide of fortune

230 **setting** set expression (of earnestness)

231 **matter** matter of importance

232 **throes** causes pain, as in giving birth.   **yield** give forth, speak about.

233–7 **although . . . alive** Although this owner of weak memory, he who will be only weakly remembered when he is dead, has nearly persuaded—since he's a mind or soul devoted solely to persuade—King Alonso that Ferdinand lives

241 **that way** i.e., in regard to Ferdinand's being saved

242–4 **that . . . there** that even ambition for high status cannot see anything higher, and even there it doubts the reality of what it sees (because the place is so supremely high). (What then follows is Antonio's analysis of why they can proceed without fear.)

SEBASTIAN   Do so. To ebb   223
  Hereditary sloth instructs me.

ANTONIO   Oh,   224
  If you but knew how you the purpose cherish   225
  Whiles thus you mock it! How, in stripping it,   226
  You more invest it! Ebbing men, indeed,   227
  Most often do so near the bottom run   228
  By their own fear or sloth.

SEBASTIAN   Prithee, say on.
  The setting of thine eye and check proclaim   230
  A matter from thee, and a birth indeed   231
  Which throes thee much to yield.

ANTONIO   Thus, sir: 232
  Although this lord of weak remembrance, this   233
  Who shall be of as little memory   234
  When he is earthed, hath here almost persuaded—   235
  For he's a spirit of persuasion, only   236
  Professes to persuade—the King his son's alive,   237
  'Tis as impossible that he's undrowned
  As he that sleeps here swims.

SEBASTIAN   I have no hope
  That he's undrowned.

ANTONIO   Oh, out of that "no hope"
  What great hope have you! No hope that way is   241
  Another way so high a hope that even   242
  Ambition cannot pierce a wink beyond,   243
  But doubt discovery there. Will you grant with me   244
  That Ferdinand is drowned?

SEBASTIAN   He's gone.

ANTONIO   Then tell me,
  Who's the next heir of Naples?

SEBASTIAN   Claribel.

ANTONIO
  She that is Queen of Tunis; she that dwells

248 **Ten . . . life** i.e., further than the journey of a lifetime

249 **note** news, intimation.   **post** messenger

251 **razorable** ready for shaving.   **from** on our voyage from

252 **cast** were disgorged. (With a pun on *casting* of parts for a play.)

255 **discharge** part to play.

259 **cubit** ancient measure of length of about twenty inches

261 **Measure us** retrace our journey.   **Keep** You, Claribel, stay

262 **wake** i.e., to his good fortune.

264 **There be** There are those

265 **prate** speak foolishly

267–8 **I . . . chat** I could teach a jackdaw to talk as wisely, or, be such a garrulous talker myself.

271–2 **And . . . fortune?** And how does your contentment with what I've just said further your good fortune?

275 **feater** more becomingly, fittingly

Ten leagues beyond man's life; she that from Naples   248
Can have no note, unless the sun were post—   249
The Man i'th' Moon's too slow—till newborn chins
Be rough and razorable; she that from whom   251
We all were sea-swallowed, though some cast again,   252
And by that destiny to perform an act
Whereof what's past is prologue, what to come
In yours and my discharge.   255

SEBASTIAN   What stuff is this? How say you?
'Tis true my brother's daughter's Queen of Tunis,
So is she heir of Naples, twixt which regions
There is some space.

ANTONIO   A space whose ev'ry cubit   259
Seems to cry out, "How shall that Claribel
Measure us back to Naples? Keep in Tunis,   261
And let Sebastian wake." Say this were death   262
That now hath seized them, why, they were no worse
Than now they are. There be that can rule Naples   264
As well as he that sleeps, lords that can prate   265
As amply and unnecessarily
As this Gonzalo. I myself could make   267
A chough of as deep chat. Oh, that you bore   268
The mind that I do! What a sleep were this
For your advancement! Do you understand me?

SEBASTIAN
Methinks I do.

ANTONIO   And how does your content   271
Tender your own good fortune?

SEBASTIAN   I remember   272
You did supplant your brother Prospero.

ANTONIO   True.
And look how well my garments sit upon me,
Much feater than before. My brother's servants   275
Were then my fellows. Now they are my men.

277 **for** as for
278 **kibe** chilblain, here a sore on the heel
279 **put me to** oblige me to wear
280–2 **Twenty . . . molest!** Even if there were twenty consciences between me and the dukedom of Milan, may they be lumped together or crystallized like candy and then melted down before I'd let them interfere!
286 **thus** similarly. (The actor makes a stabbing gesture.)
287 **wink** sleep, closing of eyes.   **aye** ever
289 **Should not** must not be allowed to
290 **take suggestion** respond to prompting
291 **tell the clock** i.e., agree, answer appropriately, chime
295 **tribute** (See 1.2.113–24.)
298 **fall it** let it fall

SEBASTIAN   But, for your conscience?   277

ANTONIO
   Ay, sir, where lies that? If 'twere a kibe,   278
   'Twould put me to my slipper; but I feel not   279
   This deity in my bosom. Twenty consciences   280
   That stand twixt me and Milan, candied be they   281
   And melt ere they molest! Here lies your brother,   282
   No better than the earth he lies upon,
   If he were that which now he's like—that's dead,
   Whom I, with this obedient steel, three inches of it,
   Can lay to bed forever; whiles you, doing thus,   286
   To the perpetual wink for aye might put   287
   This ancient morsel, this Sir Prudence, who
   Should not upbraid our course. For all the rest,   289
   They'll take suggestion as a cat laps milk;   290
   They'll tell the clock to any business that   291
   We say befits the hour.

SEBASTIAN   Thy case, dear friend,
   Shall be my precedent. As thou got'st Milan,
   I'll come by Naples. Draw thy sword. One stroke
   Shall free thee from the tribute which thou payest, 295
   And I the king shall love thee.

ANTONIO   Draw together;
   And when I rear my hand, do you the like
   To fall it on Gonzalo.   [*They draw.*]

SEBASTIAN   Oh, but one word.   298
                             [*They talk apart.*]

    Enter Ariel [invisible], with music and song.

ARIEL [*to Gonzalo*]
   My master through his art foresees the danger
   That you, his friend, are in, and sends me forth—
   For else his project dies—to keep them living.
                    Sings in Gonzalo's ear.

304 **time** opportunity
312 **securing** standing guard over
322 **cried** called out.
324 **verily** true.

> While you here do snoring lie,
> Open-eyed conspiracy
>   His time doth take.   304
> If of life you keep a care,
> Shake off slumber, and beware.
>   Awake, awake!

ANTONIO   Then let us both be sudden.

GONZALO [*waking*]   Now, good angels preserve the King!

> [*The others wake.*]

ALONSO

Why, how now, ho, awake? Why are you drawn?
Wherefore this ghastly looking?

GONZALO   What's the matter?

SEBASTIAN

Whiles we stood here securing your repose,   312
Even now, we heard a hollow burst of bellowing
Like bulls, or rather lions. Did 't not wake you?
It struck mine ear most terribly.

ALONSO   I heard nothing.

ANTONIO

Oh, 'twas a din to fright a monster's ear,
To make an earthquake! Sure it was the roar
Of a whole herd of lions.

ALONSO   Heard you this, Gonzalo?

GONZALO

Upon mine honor, sir, I heard a humming,
And that a strange one too, which did awake me.
I shaked you, sir, and cried. As mine eyes opened,   322
I saw their weapons drawn. There was a noise,
That's verily. 'Tis best we stand upon our guard,   324
Or that we quit this place. Let's draw our weapons.

ALONSO

Lead off this ground, and let's make further search
For my poor son.

2.2 *Location: Another part of the island.*

  2 **flats** swamps

  3 **By inchmeal** inch by inch

  4 **needs must** have to.   **nor** neither

  5 **urchin shows** elvish apparitions shaped like hedgehogs

  6 **like a firebrand** they in the guise of a will-o'-the-wisp

  9 **mow** make faces

13 **wound with** entwined by

17 **mind** notice

18 **bear off** keep off

GONZALO   Heavens keep him from these beasts!
　For he is, sure, i'th'island.

ALONSO   Lead away.

ARIEL [aside]
　Prospero my lord shall know what I have done.
　So, King, go safely on to seek thy son.

　　　　　　　　　　　　　　　　Exeunt [separately].

2.2 ✣ *Enter Caliban with a burden of wood. A noise*
　　　　of thunder heard.

CALIBAN
　All the infections that the sun sucks up
　From bogs, fens, flats, on Prosper fall, and make him   2
　By inchmeal a disease! His spirits hear me,   3
　And yet I needs must curse. But they'll nor pinch,   4
　Fright me with urchin shows, pitch me i'th' mire,   5
　Nor lead me, like a firebrand, in the dark   6
　Out of my way, unless he bid 'em. But
　For every trifle are they set upon me,
　Sometimes like apes, that mow and chatter at me   9
　And after bite me; then like hedgehogs, which
　Lie tumbling in my barefoot way and mount
　Their pricks at my footfall. Sometime am I
　All wound with adders, who with cloven tongues   13
　Do hiss me into madness.

　　　　　Enter Trinculo.

　　　　　　　　　Lo, now, lo!
　Here comes a spirit of his, and to torment me
　For bringing wood in slowly. I'll fall flat.
　Perchance he will not mind me.   [*He lies down.*]   17

TRINCULO Here's neither bush nor shrub to bear off   18
　any weather at all. And another storm brewing; I hear

21 **foul bombard** dirty leather jug.   **his** its

27 **Poor John** salted fish, type of poor fare.

29 **painted** i.e., painted on a sign set up outside a booth or tent at a fair

30-1 **make a man** (1) make a man's fortune (2) pass for a human being.

32 **doit** small coin

34 **o' my troth** by my faith.

35 **hold it** hold it in

38 **gaberdine** cloak, loose upper garment.

40 **shroud** take shelter

41 **dregs** i.e., last remains (as in a *bombard* or jug, line 21)

46 **swabber** crew member whose job is to wash the decks

it sing i'th' wind. Yond same black cloud, yond huge
one, looks like a foul bombard that would shed his   21
liquor. If it should thunder as it did before, I know not
where to hide my head. Yond same cloud cannot
choose but fall by pailfuls. [*Seeing Caliban*] What have
we here, a man or a fish? Dead or alive? A fish, he
smells like a fish; a very ancient and fishlike smell; a
kind of not-of-the-newest Poor John. A strange fish!   27
Were I in England now, as once I was, and had but
this fish painted, not a holiday fool there but would   29
give a piece of silver. There would this monster make   30
a man. Any strange beast there makes a man. When   31
they will not give a doit to relieve a lame beggar, they   32
will lay out ten to see a dead Indian. Legged like a
man, and his fins like arms! Warm, o' my troth! I do   34
now let loose my opinion, hold it no longer: this is no   35
fish, but an islander, that hath lately suffered by a
thunderbolt. [*Thunder.*] Alas, the storm is come again!
My best way is to creep under his gaberdine. There is   38
no other shelter hereabout. Misery acquaints a man
with strange bedfellows. I will here shroud till the   40
dregs of the storm be past.   41

> [*He creeps under Caliban's garment.*]

Enter Stephano, singing, [a bottle in his hand].

STEPHANO
> "I shall no more to sea, to sea,
> Here shall I die ashore—"

This is a very scurvy tune to sing at a man's funeral.
Well, here's my comfort.   *Drinks.*
(*Sings.*)

> "The master, the swabber, the boatswain, and I,   46
> The gunner and his mate,
> Loved Mall, Meg, and Marian, and Margery,
> But none of us cared for Kate.

50 **tang** sting

53 **tailor . . . itch** (A dig at tailors for their supposed effem-
inacy and a bawdy suggestion of satisfying a sexual crav-
ing.)

56 **Do . . . me!** (Caliban assumes that one of Prospero's
spirits has come to punish him.)

57 **What's the matter?** What's going on here?

58 **put tricks upon 's** trick us with conjuring shows.
Ind India

60 **proper** handsome

61 **four legs** (The conventional phrase would supply *two
legs*, but the creature Stephano thinks he sees has four.)

63 **at'** at the

66 **ague** fever. (Probably both Caliban and Trinculo are
quaking; see lines 56 and 81.)

67 **should he learn** could he have learned

68 **for that** i.e., for knowing our language.   **recover** revive

70–1 **neat's leather** cowhide.

74–5 **after the wisest** in the wisest fashion.

76 **afore** before.   **go near to** be in a fair way to

77 **recover** restore

77–8 **I will . . . much** i.e., no sum can be too much

78 **He shall . . . hath him** Anyone who wants him will
have to pay dearly for him

For she had a tongue with a tang,   50
Would crẏ to a sailor, 'Go hang!'
She loved not the savor of tar nor of pitch,
Yet a tailor might scratch her where'er she did itch.   53
    Then to sea, boys, and let her go hang!"
This is a scurvy tune too. But here's my comfort.

Drinks.

CALIBAN Do not torment me! Oh!   56

STEPHANO What's the matter? Have we devils here? Do   57
you put tricks upon 's with savages and men of Ind,   58
ha? I have not scaped drowning to be afeard now of
your four legs. For it hath been said, "As proper a man   60
as ever went on four legs cannot make him give   61
ground"; and it shall be said so again while Stephano
breathes at' nostrils.   63

CALIBAN This spirit torments me! Oh!

STEPHANO This is some monster of the isle with four
legs, who hath got, as I take it, an ague. Where the   66
devil should he learn our language? I will give him   67
some relief, if it be but for that. If I can recover him   68
and keep him tame and get to Naples with him, he's
a present for any emperor that ever trod on neat's   70
leather.   71

CALIBAN Do not torment me, prithee. I'll bring my
wood home faster.

STEPHANO He's in his fit now and does not talk after   74
the wisest. He shall taste of my bottle. If he have never   75
drunk wine afore, it will go near to remove his fit. If I   76
can recover him and keep him tame, I will not take too   77
much for him. He shall pay for him that hath him, and   78
that soundly.

CALIBAN Thou dost me yet but little hurt; thou wilt
anon, I know it by thy trembling. Now Prosper works
upon thee.

84–5 **cat . . . mouth** (Allusion to the proverb "Good liquor will make a cat speak.")

85 **shake** shake off

86–7 **You . . . friend** i.e., You can't tell who's your friend until someone like me provides you with a drink.

87 **chaps** jaws

90 **delicate** ingenious

92 **backward voice** (Trinculo and Caliban are facing in opposite directions. Stephano supposes the monster to have a rear end that can emit *foul speeches* or foul-smelling wind at the monster's *other mouth*, line 95.)

93 **If . . . him** Even if it takes all the wine in my bottle to cure him

99 **long spoon** (Allusion to the proverb "He that sups with the devil has need of a long spoon.")

106 **siege** excrement

107 **mooncalf** monstrous or misshapen creature (whose deformity is caused by the malignant influence of the moon). **vent** excrete, defecate

110 **overblown** blown over.

115 **constant** steady.

STEPHANO   Come on your ways. Open your mouth. Here
is that which will give language to you, cat. Open your   84
mouth. This will shake your shaking, I can tell you,   85
and that soundly. [*Giving Caliban a drink.*] You cannot   86
tell who's your friend. Open your chaps again.   87

TRINCULO   I should know that voice. It should be—but
he is drowned, and these are devils. Oh, defend me!

STEPHANO   Four legs and two voices—a most delicate   90
monster! His forward voice now is to speak well of his
friend; his backward voice is to utter foul speeches and   92
to detract. If all the wine in my bottle will recover him,   93
I will help his ague. Come. [*Giving a drink.*] Amen! I
will pour some in thy other mouth.

TRINCULO   Stephano!

STEPHANO   Doth thy other mouth call me? Mercy,
mercy! This is a devil, and no monster. I will leave
him. I have no long spoon.   99

TRINCULO   Stephano! If thou be'st Stephano, touch me
and speak to me, for I am Trinculo—be not afeard—
thy good friend Trinculo.

STEPHANO   If thou be'st Trinculo, come forth. I'll pull
thee by the lesser legs. If any be Trinculo's legs, these
are they. [*Pulling him out.*] Thou art very Trinculo
indeed! How cam'st thou to be the siege of this   106
mooncalf? Can he vent Trinculos?   107

TRINCULO   I took him to be killed with a thunderstroke.
But art thou not drowned, Stephano? I hope now thou
art not drowned. Is the storm overblown? I hid me   110
under the dead mooncalf's gaberdine for fear of the
storm. And art thou living, Stephano? Oh, Stephano,
two Neapolitans scaped!   [*He capers with Stephano.*]

STEPHANO   Prithee, do not turn me about. My stomach
is not constant.   115

116 **an if** if
117 **brave** fine, magnificent
121 **butt of sack** barrel of Canary wine
122 **by this bottle** i.e., I swear by this bottle
129 **book** i.e., bottle. (But with ironic reference to the practice of kissing the Bible in swearing an oath; see *I'll be
sworn* in line 128.)
137 **when time was** once upon a time.
139 **dog . . . bush** (The man in the moon was popularly
imagined to have with him a dog and a bush of thorn.)
142 **By . . . light** By God's light, by this good light from
heaven

CALIBAN
    These be fine things, an if they be not spirits.   116
    That's a brave god, and bears celestial liquor.   117
    I will kneel to him.

STEPHANO   How didst thou scape? How cam'st thou
hither? Swear by this bottle how thou cam'st hither. I
escaped upon a butt of sack which the sailors heaved 121
o'erboard—by this bottle, which I made of the bark of 122
a tree with mine own hands since I was cast ashore.

CALIBAN [kneeling] I'll swear upon that bottle to be
thy true subject, for the liquor is not earthly.

STEPHANO   Here. Swear then how thou escaped'st.

TRINCULO   Swum ashore, man, like a duck. I can swim
like a duck, I'll be sworn.

STEPHANO   Here, kiss the book. Though thou canst 129
swim like a duck, thou art made like a goose.

                                  [Giving him a drink.]

TRINCULO   Oh, Stephano, hast any more of this?

STEPHANO   The whole butt, man. My cellar is in a rock
by th' seaside, where my wine is hid.—How now,
mooncalf? How does thine ague?

CALIBAN   Hast thou not dropped from heaven?

STEPHANO   Out o'th' moon, I do assure thee. I was the
man i'th' moon when time was.   137

CALIBAN
    I have seen thee in her, and I do adore thee.
    My mistress showed me thee, and thy dog, and thy
      bush.   139

STEPHANO   Come, swear to that. Kiss the book. I will
furnish it anon with new contents. Swear.

                                  [Giving him a drink.]

TRINCULO   By this good light, this is a very shallow 142
monster! I afeard of him? A very weak monster! The

145 **Well . . . sooth!** Well pulled on the bottle, truly!

149 **When . . . bottle** i.e., Caliban wouldn't even stop at robbing his god (i.e., Stephano) of his bottle if he could catch him asleep.

156 **But that** were it not that.   **in drink** drunk.

165 **crabs** crab apples, or crabs

166 **pignuts** earthnuts, edible tuberous roots

168 **marmoset** small monkey.

170 **scamels** (Possibly *seamews*, mentioned in Strachey's letter, or shellfish, or perhaps from *squamelle,* "furnished with little scales." Contemporary French and Italian travel accounts report that the natives of Patagonia in South America ate small fish described as *fort scameux* and *squame.*)

man i'th' moon? A most poor credulous monster!
Well drawn, monster, in good sooth!   145

CALIBAN [to Stephano]
I'll show thee every fertile inch o'th' island,
And I will kiss thy foot. I prithee, be my god.

TRINCULO   By this light, a most perfidious and drunken
monster! When 's god's asleep, he'll rob his bottle.   149

CALIBAN
I'll kiss thy foot. I'll swear myself thy subject.

STEPHANO   Come on then. Down, and swear.

[Caliban kneels.]

TRINCULO   I shall laugh myself to death at this puppy-
headed monster. A most scurvy monster! I could find
in my heart to beat him—

STEPHANO   Come, kiss.

TRINCULO   But that the poor monster's in drink. An   156
abominable monster!

CALIBAN
I'll show thee the best springs. I'll pluck thee berries.
I'll fish for thee and get thee wood enough.
A plague upon the tyrant that I serve!
I'll bear him no more sticks, but follow thee,
Thou wondrous man.

TRINCULO   A most ridiculous monster, to make a
wonder of a poor drunkard!

CALIBAN
I prithee, let me bring thee where crabs grow,   165
And I with my long nails will dig thee pignuts,   166
Show thee a jay's nest, and instruct thee how
To snare the nimble marmoset. I'll bring thee   168
To clust'ring filberts, and sometimes I'll get thee
Young scamels from the rock. Wilt thou go with me?   170

STEPHANO   I prithee now, lead the way without any

172–3 **all . . . else** all the rest of our shipboard companions

173 **inherit** take possession

179 **firing** firewood

181 **trenchering** trenchers, wooden plates

183 **Get a new man** (Addressed to Prospero.)

184 **high-day** holiday.

3.1 *Location: Before Prospero's cell.*

1–2 **There . . . sets off** Some pastimes are laborious, but the pleasure we get from them compensates for the effort. (Pleasure is *set off* by labor as a jewel is set off by its foil.)

2 **baseness** menial activity

3 **undergone** undertaken.   **most poor** poorest

4 **mean** lowly

5 **but** were it not that

6 **quickens** give life to

11 **sore injunction** severe command.

13 **Had . . . executor** was never before undertaken by so noble a being.   **I forget** i.e., I forget that I'm supposed to be working

more talking.—Trinculo, the King and all our com- 172
pany else being drowned, we will inherit here.— 173
Here, bear my bottle.—Fellow Trinculo, we'll fill him
by and by again.

CALIBAN   (*sings drunkenly*)
Farewell, master, farewell, farewell!

TRINCULO   A howling monster; a drunken monster!

CALIBAN
No more dams I'll make for fish,
    Nor fetch in firing   179
    At requiring,
Nor scrape trenchering, nor wash dish.   181
    'Ban, 'Ban, Ca–Caliban
    Has a new master. Get a new man!   183
Freedom, high-day! High-day, freedom! Freedom,   184
high-day, freedom!

STEPHANO   O brave monster! Lead the way.   *Exeunt.*

3.1 ❧ *Enter Ferdinand, bearing a log.*

FERDINAND
There be some sports are painful, and their labor   1
Delight in them sets off. Some kinds of baseness   2
Are nobly undergone, and most poor matters   3
Point to rich ends. This my mean task   4
Would be as heavy to me as odious, but   5
The mistress which I serve quickens what's dead   6
And makes my labors pleasures. Oh, she is
Ten times more gentle than her father's crabbed,
And he's composed of harshness. I must remove
Some thousands of these logs and pile them up,
Upon a sore injunction. My sweet mistress   11
Weeps when she sees me work and says such baseness
Had never like executor. I forget;   13

15 **Most . . . do it** (Ferdinand seems to say that the busier he is, the less likely he is to forget the sweet thoughts that make his labors pleasant. The line may be in need of emendation.)

17 **enjoined** commanded

18 **this** i.e., the log

19 **weep** i.e., exude resin

21 **these** the next

22 **discharge** complete

32 **visitation** (1) Miranda's visit to Ferdinand (2) visitation of the plague, i.e., infection of love

34 **by** nearby

But these sweet thoughts do even refresh my labors,
Most busy lest when I do it.

Enter Miranda; and Prospero [at a distance,
unseen].

MIRANDA   Alas now, pray you,   15
Work not so hard. I would the lightning had
Burnt up those logs that you are enjoined to pile!   17
Pray, set it down and rest you. When this burns,   18
'Twill weep for having wearied you. My father   19
Is hard at study. Pray now, rest yourself.
He's safe for these three hours.

FERDINAND   O most dear mistress,   21
The sun will set before I shall discharge   22
What I must strive to do.

MIRANDA   If you'll sit down,
I'll bear your logs the while. Pray, give me that.
I'll carry it to the pile.

FERDINAND   No, precious creature,
I had rather crack my sinews, break my back,
Than you should such dishonor undergo
While I sit lazy by.

MIRANDA   It would become me
As well as it does you; and I should do it
With much more ease, for my good will is to it,
And yours it is against.

PROSPERO [*aside*]   Poor worm, thou art infected!
This visitation shows it.

MIRANDA   You look wearily.   32

FERDINAND
No, noble mistress, 'tis fresh morning with me
When you are by at night. I do beseech you—   34
Chiefly that I might set it in my prayers—
What is your name?

37 **hest** command.   **Admired Miranda** (Her name
    means "to be admired or wondered at.")

39 **dearest** most treasured

40 **best regard** thoughtful and approving attention

42 **diligent** attentive.   **several** various. (Also in line 43.)

45 **owed** owned

46 **put . . . foil** (1) overthrew it (as in fencing or wrestling)
    (2) served as a *foil*, or "contrast," to set it off.

48 **Of** out of

52 **How . . . abroad** What people look like in other places

53 **skilless** ignorant.   **modesty** virginity

57 **like of** be pleased with, be fond of.

58 **Something** somewhat

59 **condition** rank

61 **I would** I wish it were

62 **wooden slavery** being compelled to carry wood

62–3 **than . . . mouth** than I would allow flying insects to
    deposit their eggs in my mouth as if in decaying flesh.

MIRANDA   Miranda.—O my father,
I have broke your hest to say so.

FERDINAND   Admired Miranda!   37
Indeed the top of admiration, worth
What's dearest to the world! Full many a lady   39
I have eyed with best regard, and many a time   40
The harmony of their tongues hath into bondage
Brought my too diligent ear. For several virtues   42
Have I liked several women, never any
With so full soul but some defect in her
Did quarrel with the noblest grace she owed   45
And put it to the foil. But you, oh, you,   46
So perfect and so peerless, are created
Of every creature's best!

MIRANDA   I do not know   48
One of my sex; no woman's face remember,
Save, from my glass, mine own. Nor have I seen
More that I may call men than you, good friend,
And my dear father. How features are abroad   52
I am skilless of; but, by my modesty,   53
The jewel in my dower, I would not wish
Any companion in the world but you;
Nor can imagination form a shape,
Besides yourself, to like of. But I prattle   57
Something too wildly, and my father's precepts   58
I therein do forget.

FERDINAND   I am in my condition   59
A prince, Miranda; I do think, a king—
I would, not so!—and would no more endure   61
This wooden slavery than to suffer   62
The flesh-fly blow my mouth. Hear my soul speak: 63
The very instant that I saw you did
My heart fly to your service, there resides
To make me slave to it, and for your sake
Am I this patient log-man.

69 **kind event** favorable outcome

70 **hollowly** insincerely, falsely.   **invert** turn

71 **boded** in store for.   **mischief** harm.

72 **what** whatever

79 **die** (Probably with an unconscious sexual meaning that underlies all of lines 77–81.)   **to want** through lacking.

81 **bashful cunning** coyness

84 **maid** handmaiden, servant.   **fellow** mate

86 **will** desire it.   **My mistress** i.e., The woman I adore and serve (not an illicit sexual partner)

89 **willing** desirous

MIRANDA   Do you love me?

FERDINAND
O heaven, O earth, bear witness to this sound,
And crown what I profess with kind event   69
If I speak true! If hollowly, invert   70
What best is boded me to mischief! I   71
Beyond all limit of what else i'th' world   72
Do love, prize, honor you.

MIRANDA [*weeping*]   I am a fool
To weep at what I am glad of.

PROSPERO [*aside*]   Fair encounter
Of two most rare affections! Heavens rain grace
On that which breeds between 'em!

FERDINAND   Wherefore weep you?

MIRANDA
At mine unworthiness, that dare not offer
What I desire to give, and much less take
What I shall die to want. But this is trifling,   79
And all the more it seeks to hide itself
The bigger bulk it shows. Hence, bashful cunning, 81
And prompt me, plain and holy innocence!
I am your wife, if you will marry me;
If not, I'll die your maid. To be your fellow   84
You may deny me, but I'll be your servant
Whether you will or no.

FERDINAND   My mistress, dearest,   86
And I thus humble ever.

MIRANDA   My husband, then?

FERDINAND   Ay, with a heart as willing   89
As bondage e'er of freedom. Here's my hand.

MIRANDA [*clasping his hand*]
And mine, with my heart in't. And now farewell

92 **A thousand thousand!** A thousand thousand farewells!

94 **with all** by everything that has happened, or, *withal,*
"by it"

97 **appertaining** related to this.

3.2 *Location: Another part of the island.*

1 **out** empty

2–3 **bear . . . 'em** (Stephano uses the terminology of ma-
neuvering at sea and boarding a vessel under attack as a
way of urging an assault on the liquor supply.)

4 **folly of** i.e., stupidity found on

6 **be brained** are endowed with intelligence

9 **set . . . head** fixed in a drunken stare. (But Trinculo answers in a literal sense.)

10 **set** placed

11 **brave** fine, splendid

13 **sack** Spanish wine. (Also in line 28.)

14 **recover** gain, reach

14–15 **five . . . on** i.e., a little over a hundred miles, give or
take, or, off and on, intermittently. (A drunken hyper-
bole.)

15 **By this light** (An oath: By the light of the sun.)

16 **standard** standard-bearer, ensign. (But Trinculo answers in the literal sense: Caliban is *no standard,* not able
to stand up because he's so drunk.)

17 **list** prefer

18 **run** run away, retreat (as a standard-bearer should not
do)

19 **Nor . . . dogs** i.e., You won't even walk, much less run;
you'll lie down in the field like the proverbial cowardly
dog. (With a play on *lie,* tell falsehoods.)

Till half an hour hence.

FERDINAND   A thousand thousand!   92

        Exeunt [Ferdinand and Miranda, separately].

PROSPERO

So glad of this as they I cannot be,
Who are surprised with all; but my rejoicing   94
At nothing can be more. I'll to my book,
For yet ere suppertime must I perform
Much business appertaining.   *Exit.*   97

3.2 ⤳ *Enter Caliban, Stephano, and Trinculo.*

STEPHANO   Tell not me. When the butt is out, we will   1
  drink water, not a drop before. Therefore bear up and   2
  board 'em. Servant monster, drink to me.   3

TRINCULO   Servant monster? The folly of this island!   4
  They say there's but five upon this isle. We are three
  of them; if th'other two be brained like us, the state   6
  totters.

STEPHANO   Drink, servant monster, when I bid thee.
  Thy eyes are almost set in thy head.   [*Giving a drink.*]   9

TRINCULO   Where should they be set else? He were a   10
  brave monster indeed if they were set in his tail.   11

STEPHANO   My man-monster hath drowned his tongue
  in sack. For my part, the sea cannot drown me. I   13
  swam, ere I could recover the shore, five and thirty   14
  leagues off and on. By this light, thou shalt be my   15
  lieutenant, monster, or my standard.   16

TRINCULO   Your lieutenant, if you list; he's no standard.   17

STEPHANO   We'll not run, Monsieur Monster.   18

TRINCULO   Nor go neither, but you'll lie like dogs and   19
  yet say nothing neither.

STEPHANO   Mooncalf, speak once in thy life, if thou
  be'st a good mooncalf.

25–6 **in case** ready, valiant enough

26 **deboshed** debauched, drunken

27 **ever . . . coward** ever a coward. (Trinculo appeals to his gargantuan drinking as refutation of the charge that he is *not valiant*, line 24.)

32 **natural** fool, idiot.

35 **the next tree** i.e., you'll hang.

39 **Marry** i.e., Indeed. (Originally an oath, "by the Virgin Mary.")

40.1 *invisible* i.e., wearing a garment to connote invisibility, as at 1.2.377.2.

48 **supplant** uproot, displace

CALIBAN
How does Thy Honor? Let me lick thy shoe.
I'll not serve him. He is not valiant.

TRINCULO   Thou liest, most ignorant monster, I am in   25
case to jostle a constable. Why, thou deboshed fish,   26
thou, was there ever man a coward that hath drunk so   27
much sack as I today? Wilt thou tell a monstrous lie,
being but half a fish and half a monster?

CALIBAN
Lo, how he mocks me! Wilt thou let him, my lord?

TRINCULO   "Lord," quoth he? That a monster should be
such a natural!   32

CALIBAN
Lo, lo, again! Bite him to death, I prithee.

STEPHANO   Trinculo, keep a good tongue in your head.
If you prove a mutineer—the next tree! The poor mon-   35
ster's my subject, and he shall not suffer indignity.

CALIBAN
I thank my noble lord. Wilt thou be pleased
To hearken once again to the suit I made to thee?

STEPHANO   Marry, will I. Kneel and repeat it. I will   39
stand, and so shall Trinculo.   [Caliban kneels.]   40

        Enter Ariel, invisible.

CALIBAN
As I told thee before, I am subject to a tyrant,
A sorcerer, that by his cunning hath
Cheated me of the island.

ARIEL [mimicking Trinculo]
Thou liest.

CALIBAN   Thou liest, thou jesting monkey, thou!
I would my valiant master would destroy thee.
I do not lie.

STEPHANO   Trinculo, if you trouble him any more in 's
tale, by this hand, I will supplant some of your teeth.   48

54 **this thing** i.e., Trinculo

57 **compassed** achieved.

62 **pied ninny** fool in motley.   **patch** fool.

66 **quick freshes** running springs

69 **turn . . . o' doors** banish all merciful feelings.
     stockfish dried cod beaten before cooking

76 **give me the lie** call me a liar to my face

TRINCULO   Why, I said nothing.

STEPHANO   Mum, then, and no more.—Proceed.

CALIBAN
I say by sorcery he got this isle;
From me he got it. If Thy Greatness will
Revenge it on him—for I know thou dar'st,
But this thing dare not—   54

STEPHANO   That's most certain.

CALIBAN
Thou shalt be lord of it, and I'll serve thee.

STEPHANO   How now shall this be compassed? Canst 57
thou bring me to the party?

CALIBAN
Yea, yea, my lord. I'll yield him thee asleep,
Where thou mayst knock a nail into his head.

ARIEL [mimicking Trinculo]   Thou liest; thou canst not.

CALIBAN
What a pied ninny's this! Thou scurvy patch!—   62
I do beseech Thy Greatness, give him blows
And take his bottle from him. When that's gone
He shall drink naught but brine, for I'll not show
    him
Where the quick freshes are.   66

STEPHANO   Trinculo, run into no further danger. Interrupt the monster one word further and, by this hand,
I'll turn my mercy out o' doors and make a stockfish of 69
thee.

TRINCULO   Why, what did I? I did nothing. I'll go farther
off.

STEPHANO   Didst thou not say he lied?

ARIEL [mimicking Trinculo]   Thou liest.

STEPHANO   Do I so? Take thou that.   [He beats Trinculo.]
As you like this, give me the lie another time.   76

78 **A pox** i.e., A plague. (A curse.)
79 **murrain** plague. (Literally, a cattle disease.)
90 **paunch** stab in the belly
91 **weasand** windpipe
93 **sot** fool
96 **brave utensils** fine furnishings
97 **deck withal** furnish it with.
104 **brave** splendid, attractive
105 **become** suit (sexually)

TRINCULO   I did not give the lie. Out o' your wits and
   hearing too? A pox o' your bottle! This can sack and   78
   drinking do. A murrain on your monster, and the   79
   devil take your fingers!

CALIBAN   Ha, ha, ha!

STEPHANO   Now, forward with your tale.   [To Trinculo]
   Prithee, stand further off.

CALIBAN
   Beat him enough. After a little time
   I'll beat him too.

STEPHANO   Stand farther.—Come, proceed.

CALIBAN
   Why, as I told thee, 'tis a custom with him
   I'th'afternoon to sleep. There thou mayst brain him,
   Having first seized his books; or with a log
   Batter his skull, or paunch him with a stake,   90
   Or cut his weasand with thy knife. Remember   91
   First to possess his books, for without them
   He's but a sot, as I am, nor hath not   93
   One spirit to command. They all do hate him
   As rootedly as I. Burn but his books.
   He has brave utensils—for so he calls them—   96
   Which, when he has a house, he'll deck withal.   97
   And that most deeply to consider is
   The beauty of his daughter. He himself
   Calls her a nonpareil. I never saw a woman
   But only Sycorax my dam and she;
   But she as far surpasseth Sycorax
   As great'st does least.

STEPHANO   Is it so brave a lass?   104

CALIBAN
   Ay, lord. She will become thy bed, I warrant,   105
   And bring thee forth brave brood.

STEPHANO   Monster, I will kill this man. His daughter

119 **jocund** jovial, merry.   **troll the catch** sing the round

120 **but whilere** only a short time ago.

121–2 **reason, any reason** anything reasonable.

123 **Flout** Scoff at.   **scout** deride

126.1 *tabor* small drum

129 **picture of Nobody** (Refers to a familiar figure with head, arms, and legs but no trunk.)

131 **take't . . . list** (A proverbial formula of bravado and defiance, as in *Romeo and Juliet*, 1.1.40–1.)

133 **He . . . debts** (Another proverbial swagger: Death settles all scores, I'm not afraid to fight.)

and I will be king and queen—save Our Graces!—and
Trinculo and thyself shall be viceroys. Dost thou like
the plot, Trinculo?

TRINCULO Excellent.

STEPHANO Give me thy hand. I am sorry I beat thee;
but, while thou liv'st, keep a good tongue in thy head.

CALIBAN
Within this half hour will he be asleep.
Wilt thou destroy him then?

STEPHANO Ay, on mine honor.

ARIEL [aside] This will I tell my master.

CALIBAN
Thou mak'st me merry; I am full of pleasure.
Let us be jocund. Will you troll the catch   119
You taught me but whilere?   120

STEPHANO At thy request, monster, I will do reason, 121
any reason.—Come on, Trinculo, let us sing. *Sings.* 122
  "Flout 'em and scout 'em   123
  And scout 'em and flout 'em!
    Thought is free."

CALIBAN That's not the tune.   126

                Ariel plays the tune on a tabor and pipe.

STEPHANO What is this same?

TRINCULO This is the tune of our catch, played by the
picture of Nobody.   129

STEPHANO If thou be'st a man, show thyself in thy
likeness. If thou be'st a devil, take't as thou list. 131

TRINCULO Oh, forgive me my sins!

STEPHANO He that dies pays all debts. I defy thee. 133
Mercy upon us!

CALIBAN Art thou afeard?

STEPHANO No, monster, not I.

145 **to dream** desirous of dreaming
149 **by and by** very soon.
154 **lays it on** i.e., plays the drum vigorously.

3.3 *Location: Another part of the island.*
1 **By'r lakin** By our Ladykin, by our Lady
3 **forthrights and meanders** paths straight and crooked.
5 **attached with** seized by
6 **To . . . spirits** to the point of being dull-spirited.

CALIBAN
    Be not afeard. The isle is full of noises,
    Sounds, and sweet airs, that give delight and hurt not.
    Sometimes a thousand twangling instruments
    Will hum about mine ears, and sometimes voices
    That, if I then had waked after long sleep,
    Will make me sleep again; and then, in dreaming,
    The clouds methought would open and show riches
    Ready to drop upon me, that when I waked
    I cried to dream again.   • 145

STEPHANO   This will prove a brave kingdom to me,
    where I shall have my music for nothing.

CALIBAN   When Prospero is destroyed.

STEPHANO   That shall be by and by. I remember the 149
    story.

TRINCULO   The sound is going away. Let's follow it,
    and after do our work.

STEPHANO   Lead, monster; we'll follow. I would I could
    see this taborer! He lays it on.   154

TRINCULO   Wilt come? I'll follow, Stephano.

                    Exeunt [following Ariel's music].

3.3 ❧ *Enter Alonso, Sebastian, Antonio, Gonzalo,*
    Adrian, Francisco, etc.

GONZALO
    By'r lakin, I can go no further, sir.   1
    My old bones aches. Here's a maze trod indeed
    Through forthrights and meanders! By your patience, 3
    I needs must rest me.

ALONSO   Old lord, I cannot blame thee,
    Who am myself attached with weariness,   5
    To th' dulling of my spirits. Sit down and rest.   6
    Even here I will put off my hope, and keep it

10 **frustrate** frustrated

12 **for** because of

14 **throughly** thoroughly.

15 **now** now that.   **travel** (Spelled "trauaile" in the Folio and carrying the sense of labor as well as traveling.)

16 **use such vigilance** be as vigilant

17.1–2 ***on the top*** at some high point of the tiring-house or the theater, on a third level above the gallery

20 **kind keepers** guardian angels

21 **living drollery** comic entertainment, caricature, or puppet show put on by live actors.

23 **phoenix** mythical bird consumed to ashes every five hundred to six hundred years, only to be renewed into another cycle

25 **want credit** lack credibility

No longer for my flatterer. He is drowned
Whom thus we stray to find, and the sea mocks
Our frustrate search on land. Well, let him go.   10

                        [*Alonso and Gonzalo sit.*]

ANTONIO [*aside to Sebastian*]
I am right glad that he's so out of hope.
Do not, for one repulse, forgo the purpose   12
That you resolved t'effect.

SEBASTIAN [*to Antonio*]   The next advantage
Will we take throughly.

ANTONIO [*to Sebastian*]   Let it be tonight,   14
For, now they are oppressed with travel, they   15
Will not, nor cannot, use such vigilance   16
As when they are fresh.

SEBASTIAN [*to Antonio*]   I say tonight. No more.   17

             Solemn and strange music; and Prospero on
             the top, invisible.

ALONSO
What harmony is this? My good friends, hark!

GONZALO   Marvelous sweet music!

             Enter several strange shapes, bringing in a ban-
             quet, and dance about it with gentle actions of
             salutations; and, inviting the King, etc., to eat,
             they depart.

ALONSO
Give us kind keepers, heavens! What were these?   20

SEBASTIAN
A living drollery. Now I will believe   21
That there are unicorns; that in Arabia
There is one tree, the phoenix' throne, one phoenix   23
At this hour reigning there.

ANTONIO   I'll believe both;
And what does else want credit, come to me   25

30 **certes** certainly

36 **muse** wonder at

38 **want** lack

39 **Praise in departing** i.e., Save your praise until the end of the performance. (Proverbial.)

41 **viands** provisions.   **stomachs** appetites.

44 **mountaineers** mountain dwellers

45 **Dewlapped** having a dewlap, or fold of skin hanging from the neck, like cattle

46 **Wallets** pendent folds of skin, wattles

47 **in their breasts** (i.e., like the Anthropophagi described in *Othello*, 1.3.146.)

And I'll be sworn 'tis true. Travelers ne'er did lie,
Though fools at home condemn 'em.

GONZALO   If in Naples
I should report this now, would they believe me
If I should say I saw such islanders?
For, certes, these are people of the island,   30
Who, though they are of monstrous shape, yet note,
Their manners are more gentle, kind, than of
Our human generation you shall find
Many, nay, almost any.

PROSPERO [aside]   Honest lord,
Thou hast said well, for some of you there present
Are worse than devils.

ALONSO   I cannot too much muse   36
Such shapes, such gesture, and such sound,
    expressing—
Although they want the use of tongue—a kind   38
Of excellent dumb discourse.

PROSPERO [aside]   Praise in departing.   39

FRANCISCO
They vanished strangely.

SEBASTIAN   No matter, since
They have left their viands behind, for we have
    stomachs.   41
Will 't please you taste of what is here?

ALONSO   Not I.

GONZALO
Faith, sir, you need not fear. When we were boys,
Who would believe that there were mountaineers   44
Dewlapped like bulls, whose throats had hanging at
    'em   45
Wallets of flesh? Or that there were such men   46
Whose heads stood in their breasts? Which now we
    find   47

48 **putter-out . . . one** one who invests money or gambles on the risks of travel on the condition that the traveler who returns safely is to receive five times the amount deposited; hence, any traveler

49 **Good warrant** assurance.   **stand to** come forward, fall to. (Also in line 52.)

50 **Although my last** even if this were to be my last meal

51 **best** best part of life

52.1 *harpy* a fabulous monster with a woman's face and breasts and a vulture's body, supposed to be a minister of divine vengeance

52.2–3 *with . . . vanishes* by means of some ingenious stage contrivance, the food vanishes. (The table remains until line 82.)

53–6 **whom . . . up you** you whom Destiny, acting through this sublunary world as its instrument, has caused the ever-hungry sea to belch up

59 **suchlike valor** i.e., the reckless valor derived from madness

60 **proper** own

62 **whom** which.   **tempered** made hard

63 **bemocked-at** scorned

64 **still-closing** always closing again when parted

65 **dowl** soft, fine feather

66 **like** likewise, similarly.   **If** Even if

67 **massy** heavy

71 **requit** requited, avenged

Each putter-out of five for one will bring us   48
Good warrant of.

ALONSO   I will stand to and feed,   49
Although my last—no matter, since I feel   50
The best is past. Brother, my lord the Duke,   51
Stand to, and do as we.   [*They approach the table.*]   52

> *Thunder and lightning. Enter Ariel, like a harpy,*
> *claps his wings upon the table, and with a quaint*
> *device the banquet vanishes.*

ARIEL

You are three men of sin, whom Destiny—   53
That hath to instrument this lower world   54
And what is in't—the never-surfeited sea   55
Hath caused to belch up you, and on this island   56
Where man doth not inhabit, you 'mongst men
Being most unfit to live. I have made you mad;
And even with suchlike valor men hang and drown   59
Their proper selves.   [*Alonso, Sebastian, and Antonio*
                                                                     draw their swords.]
                                   You fools! I and my fellows   60
Are ministers of Fate. The elements
Of whom your swords are tempered may as well   62
Wound the loud winds, or with bemocked-at stabs   63
Kill the still-closing waters, as diminish   64
One dowl that's in my plume. My fellow ministers   65
Are like invulnerable. If you could hurt,   66
Your swords are now too massy for your strengths   67
And will not be uplifted. But remember—
For that's my business to you—that you three
From Milan did supplant good Prospero;
Exposed unto the sea, which hath requit it,   71
Him and his innocent child; for which foul deed
The powers, delaying, not forgetting, have
Incensed the seas and shores, yea, all the creatures,

77 **perdition** ruin, destruction

79 **whose . . . from** to guard you from which heavenly wrath

80 **else** otherwise

81 **is nothing** there is no way

82 **clear** unspotted, innocent

82.2–3 *mocks and mows* mocking gestures and grimaces

83 **Bravely** Finely, dashingly

84 **a grace . . . devouring** your impersonation displayed a ravishing grace. (With a punning suggestion of having caused the banquet to disappear as if by consuming it.)

85 **bated** abated, omitted

86–8 **So . . . done** Similarly, my lesser spirits assisting you have done their various tasks with observant care and attention to detail.

90 **distractions** trancelike state.

94–5 **why . . . stare?** (Gonzalo was not addressed in Ariel's speech to the *three men of sin*, line 53, and is not, as they are, in a maddened state; see lines 105–7.)

95 **it** i.e., my sin. (Also in line 96.)

96 **billows** waves

99 **bass my trespass** proclaim my trespass like a bass note in the music.

Against your peace. Thee of thy son, Alonso,
They have bereft; and do pronounce by me
Ling'ring perdition, worse than any death   77
Can be at once, shall step by step attend
You and your ways; whose wraths to guard you
   from—   79
Which here, in this most desolate isle, else falls   80
Upon your heads—is nothing but heart's sorrow   81
And a clear life ensuing.   82

    He vanishes in thunder; then, to soft music,
    enter the shapes again, and dance, with mocks
    and mows, and carrying out the table.

PROSPERO
  Bravely the figure of this harpy hast thou   83
  Performed, my Ariel; a grace it had devouring.   84
  Of my instruction hast thou nothing bated   85
  In what thou hadst to say. So, with good life   86
  And observation strange, my meaner ministers   87
  Their several kinds have done. My high charms work,   88
  And these mine enemies are all knit up
  In their distractions. They now are in my power;   90
  And in these fits I leave them, while I visit
  Young Ferdinand, whom they suppose is drowned,
  And his and mine loved darling.   [*Exit above.*]

GONZALO
  I'th' name of something holy, sir, why stand you   94
  In this strange stare?

ALONSO   Oh, it is monstrous, monstrous!   95
  Methought the billows spoke and told me of it;   96
  The winds did sing it to me, and the thunder,
  That deep and dreadful organ pipe, pronounced
  The name of Prosper; it did bass my trespass.   99
  Therefor my son i'th'ooze is bedded; and

101 **than . . . sounded** than ever a lead weight attached to a line tested the depth

103–4 **But . . . o'er** If the demons come at me one at a time, I'll fight them all.

105 **desperate** despairing and reckless.

106 **Like . . . after** like poison, starting to work long after it has been administered

107 **bite the spirits** sap their vital powers through anguish.

107–8 **you . . . joints** Adrian, Francisco, and others not under Ariel's numbing spell

109 **ecstasy** mad frenzy

4.1 *Location: Before Prospero's cell.*

3 **a third** i.e., Miranda, into whose education I have put a third of my life, or (less precisely) who represents a large part of what I have cared about, along with my dukedom and my magical art

5 **tender** offer

7 **strangely** exceptionally

9 **boast her off** i.e., praise her so, or, perhaps an error for "boast of her"; the Folio reads "boast her of"

11 **halt** limp

12 **Against an oracle** even if an oracle should declare otherwise.

I'll seek him deeper than e'er plummet sounded,   101
And with him there lie mudded.   *Exit.*

SEBASTIAN   But one fiend at a time,   103
I'll fight their legions o'er.

ANTONIO   I'll be thy second.   104
                    Exeunt [Sebastian and Antonio].

GONZALO
All three of them are desperate. Their great guilt,   105
Like poison given to work a great time after,   106
Now 'gins to bite the spirits. I do beseech you,   107
That are of suppler joints, follow them swiftly   108
And hinder them from what this ecstasy   109
May now provoke them to.

ADRIAN   Follow, I pray you.
                    Exeunt omnes.

4.1 ᵔᵔᵔ *Enter Prospero, Ferdinand, and Miranda.*

PROSPERO
If I have too austerely punished you,
Your compensation makes amends, for I
Have given you here a third of mine own life,   3
Or that for which I live; who once again
I tender to thy hand. All thy vexations   5
Were but my trials of thy love, and thou
Hast strangely stood the test. Here, afore heaven,   7
I ratify this my rich gift. O Ferdinand,
Do not smile at me that I boast her off,   9
For thou shalt find she will outstrip all praise
And make it halt behind her.

FERDINAND   I do believe it   11
Against an oracle.   12

PROSPERO
Then, as my gift and thine own acquisition

16 **sanctimonious** sacred

18 **aspersion** dew, shower

21 **weeds** (In place of the flowers customarily strewn on the marriage bed.)

23 **As . . . you** i.e., as you long for happiness and concord in your marriage. (Hymen was the Greek and Roman god of marriage; his symbolic torches, the wedding torches, were supposed to burn brightly for a happy marriage and smokily for a troubled one.)

24 **issue** offspring

26–7 **the strong'st . . . can** the strongest temptation that the evil spirit within us can propose

28 **to** so as to

29 **edge** keen enjoyment, sexual ardor

30 **or . . . foundered** either that the horses of the sun's chariot have gone lame (thus delaying the night for which I will be so eager)

33 **What** Now then

35 **meaner fellows** subordinates

37 **trick** device.   **rabble** band, i.e., the *meaner fellows* of line 35

Worthily purchased, take my daughter. But
If thou dost break her virgin-knot before
All sanctimonious ceremonies may   16
With full and holy rite be ministered,
No sweet aspersion shall the heavens let fall   18
To make this contract grow; but barren hate,
Sour-eyed disdain, and discord shall bestrew
The union of your bed with weeds so loathly   21
That you shall hate it both. Therefore take heed,
As Hymen's lamps shall light you.

FERDINAND   As I hope   23
For quiet days, fair issue, and long life,   24
With such love as 'tis now, the murkiest den,
The most opportune place, the strong'st suggestion   26
Our worser genius can, shall never melt   27
Mine honor into lust, to take away   28
The edge of that day's celebration   29
When I shall think or Phoebus' steeds are foundered   30
Or Night kept chained below.

PROSPERO   Fairly spoke.
Sit then and talk with her. She is thine own.
          [*Ferdinand and Miranda sit and talk together.*]
What, Ariel! My industrious servant, Ariel!   33

       Enter Ariel.

ARIEL
What would my potent master? Here I am.

PROSPERO
Thou and thy meaner fellows your last service   35
Did worthily perform, and I must use you
In such another trick. Go bring the rabble,   37
O'er whom I give thee power, here to this place.
Incite them to quick motion, for I must
Bestow upon the eyes of this young couple

41 **vanity** (1) illusion (2) trifle (3) desire for admiration, conceit

42 **Presently?** Immediately?

43 **with a twink** in the twinkling of an eye.

47 **mop and mow** grimaces.

50 **conceive** understand.

51 **true** true to your promise

54 **good night** i.e., say good-bye to.   **warrant** guarantee

55 **The white . . . heart** i.e., the chaste ideal to which my heart is devoted

56 **liver** (The presumed seat of the passions.)

57 **corollary** surplus, extra supply

58 **want** lack.   **pertly** briskly.

59 **No tongue!** Quiet, everyone!

59.1 *Iris* goddess of the rainbow and Juno's messenger.

60 **Ceres** goddess of the generative power of nature. **leas** meadows

61 **vetches** plants for forage, fodder

63 **meads** meadows.   **stover** winter fodder for cattle

64 **pionèd and twillèd** undercut by the swift current and protected by roots and branches that tangle to form a barricade

Some vanity of mine art. It is my promise, 41
And they expect it from me.

ARIEL   Presently? 42

PROSPERO   Ay, with a twink. 43

ARIEL
Before you can say "Come" and "Go,"
And breathe twice, and cry "So, so,"
Each one, tripping on his toe,
Will be here with mop and mow. 47
Do you love me, master? No?

PROSPERO
Dearly, my delicate Ariel. Do not approach
Till thou dost hear me call.

ARIEL   Well; I conceive.   *Exit.* 50

PROSPERO
Look thou be true; do not give dalliance 51
Too much the rein. The strongest oaths are straw
To th' fire i'th' blood. Be more abstemious,
Or else good night your vow!

FERDINAND   I warrant you, sir, 54
The white cold virgin snow upon my heart 55
Abates the ardor of my liver.

PROSPERO   Well. 56
Now come, my Ariel! Bring a corollary, 57
Rather than want a spirit. Appear, and pertly!— 58
No tongue! All eyes! Be silent.   *Soft music.* 59

        Enter Iris.

IRIS
Ceres, most bounteous lady, thy rich leas 60
Of wheat, rye, barley, vetches, oats, and peas; 61
Thy turfy mountains, where live nibbling sheep,
And flat meads thatched with stover, them to keep; 63
Thy banks with pionèd and twillèd brims, 64

65 **spongy** wet.   **hest** command

66 **broom groves** clumps of broom, gorse, yellow-flowered shrub

67 **dismissèd bachelor** rejected male lover

68 **poll-clipped** pruned, lopped at the top, or *pole-clipped*, "hedged in with poles"

69 **sea marge** shore

70 **thou . . . air** you take the air, go for walks.   **queen o'th' sky** i.e., Juno

71 **wat'ry arch** rainbow

72.1 *Juno descends* i.e., starts her descent from the "heavens" above the stage

74 **peacocks** birds sacred to Juno and used to pull her chariot.   **amain** with full speed.

75 **entertain** receive.

78 **saffron** yellow

80 **bow** rainbow

81 **bosky** wooded.   **unshrubbed down** open upland

82 **scarf** (The rainbow is like a colored silk band adorning the earth.)

85 **estate** bestow

87 **son** i.e., Cupid.   **as** as far as

88–91 **Since . . . forsworn** Since Venus and her blind son Cupid plotted the means by which Dis (Pluto) carried off my daughter Proserpina to be his bride in Hades, I have forsworn their scandalous company.

Which spongy April at thy hest betrims   65
To make cold nymphs chaste crowns; and thy
   broom groves,   66
Whose shadow the dismissèd bachelor loves,   67
Being lass-lorn; thy poll-clipped vineyard;   68
And thy sea marge, sterile and rocky hard,   69
Where thou thyself dost air: the queen o'th' sky,   70
Whose wat'ry arch and messenger am I,   71
Bids thee leave these, and with her sovereign grace,   72

       Juno descends [slowly in her car].

Here on this grass plot, in this very place,
To come and sport. Her peacocks fly amain.   74
Approach, rich Ceres, her to entertain.   75

   Enter Ceres.

CERES
Hail, many-colored messenger, that ne'er
Dost disobey the wife of Jupiter,
Who with thy saffron wings upon my flowers   78
Diffusest honeydrops, refreshing showers,
And with each end of thy blue bow dost crown   80
My bosky acres and my unshrubbed down,   81
Rich scarf to my proud earth. Why hath thy queen   82
Summoned me hither to this short-grassed green?

IRIS
A contract of true love to celebrate,
And some donation freely to estate   85
On the blest lovers.

CERES   Tell me, heavenly bow,
If Venus or her son, as thou dost know,   87
Do now attend the Queen? Since they did plot   88
The means that dusky Dis my daughter got,   89
Her and her blind boy's scandaled company   90
I have forsworn.

IRIS   Of her society   91

92 **Her Deity** i.e., Her Highness

93 **Paphos** place on the island of Cyprus, sacred to Venus

94 **Dove-drawn** (Venus's chariot was drawn by doves.)

94–5 **done . . . charm** inflicted some lustful spell

96 **that . . . paid** that their union will not be sexually consummated

98 **Mars's hot minion** i.e., Venus, the beloved of Mars. **returned** i.e., returned to Paphos

99 **waspish-headed** hotheaded, peevish

100 **sparrows** (Supposed lustful, and sacred to Venus.)

101 **right out** outright.　　**Highest . . . state** Most majestic Queen

102 **gait** i.e., majestic bearing.

103 **sister** i.e., fellow goddess.

105 **issue** offspring.

108 **still** aways

110 **foison plenty** plentiful harvest

111 **garners** granaries

115 **In . . . harvest** i.e., with no winter in between.

Be not afraid. I met Her Deity   92
Cutting the clouds towards Paphos, and her son   93
Dove-drawn with her. Here thought they to have
    done   94
Some wanton charm upon this man and maid,   95
Whose vows are that no bed-right shall be paid   96
Till Hymen's torch be lighted; but in vain.
Mars's hot minion is returned again;   98
Her waspish-headed son has broke his arrows,   99
Swears he will shoot no more, but play with
    sparrows   100
And be a boy right out.

    [Juno alights.]

CERES   Highest Queen of state,   101
   Great Juno, comes; I know her by her gait.   102

JUNO
   How does my bounteous sister? Go with me   103
   To bless this twain, that they may prosperous be,
   And honored in their issue.   *They sing:* 105

JUNO
    Honor, riches, marriage blessing,
    Long continuance, and increasing,
    Hourly joys be still upon you!   108
    Juno sings her blessings on you.

CERES
    Earth's increase, foison plenty,   110
    Barns and garners never empty,   111
    Vines with clust'ring bunches growing,
    Plants with goodly burden bowing;

    Spring come to you at the farthest
    In the very end of harvest!   115

119 **charmingly** enchantingly.

123 **wondered** wonder-performing, wondrous.   **wise**
(The Folio appears to read "wise" here, but with a tall
"s" that resembles an "f," leading to much dispute over
this reading. In some copies of the Folio the "s" looks
like an "f," perhaps damaged, but evidently as the result of an inkblot, so that the true reading is "s." Even
so, an error in transmission would be easy, so that the
author's intention is uncertain. The matter bears im-
portantly on whether or not Ferdinand includes
Miranda in his vision of paradise.)

128 **naiads** nymphs of springs, rivers, or lakes.   **windring** wandering, winding (?)

129 **sedged** made of reeds.   **ever-harmless** ever innocent

130 **crisp** curled, rippled

132 **temperate** chaste

134 **sicklemen** harvesters, field workers who cut down
grain and grass.   **of August weary** i.e., weary of
the hard work of the harvest

135 **furrow** i.e., plowed fields

137 **encounter** join

138 **country footing** country dancing.

138.1 *properly* suitably

Scarcity and want shall shun you;
Ceres' blessing so is on you.

FERDINAND
This is a most majestic vision, and
Harmonious charmingly. May I be bold   119
To think these spirits?

PROSPERO   Spirits, which by mine art
I have from their confines called to enact
My present fancies.

FERDINAND   Let me live here ever!
So rare a wondered father and a wise   123
Makes this place Paradise.

Juno and Ceres whisper, and send
Iris on employment.

PROSPERO   Sweet now, silence!
Juno and Ceres whisper seriously;
There's something else to do. Hush and be mute,
Or else our spell is marred.

IRIS [*calling offstage*]
You nymphs, called naiads, of the windring brooks,   128
With your sedged crowns and ever-harmless looks,   129
Leave your crisp channels, and on this green land   130
Answer your summons; Juno does command.
Come, temperate nymphs, and help to celebrate   132
A contract of true love. Be not too late.

Enter certain nymphs.

You sunburned sicklemen, of August weary,   134
Come hither from the furrow and be merry.   135
Make holiday; your rye-straw hats put on,
And these fresh nymphs encounter every one   137
In country footing.   138

Enter certain reapers, properly habited. They join
with the nymphs in a graceful dance, towards the

138.5 *heavily* slowly, dejectedly

142 **Avoid** Withdraw

144 **works** affects, agitates

146 **moved sort** troubled state, condition

148 **revels** entertainment, pageant

151 **baseless fabric** unsubstantial theatrical edifice or contrivance

153 **great globe** (With a glance at the Globe Theatre.)

154 **which it inherit** who subsequently occupy it

156 **rack** wisp of cloud

157 **on** of

158 **rounded** surrounded (before birth and after death), or
crowned, rounded off

160 **with** by

161 **retire** withdraw, go

163 **beating** agitated

end whereof Prospero starts suddenly, and speaks;
after which, to a strange, hollow, and confused
noise, they heavily vanish.

PROSPERO [*aside*]
  I had forgot that foul conspiracy
  Of the beast Caliban and his confederates
  Against my life. The minute of their plot
  Is almost come. [*To the Spirits*] Well done! Avoid; no
      more!   142

FERDINAND [*to Miranda*]
  This is strange. Your father's in some passion
  That works him strongly.

MIRANDA   Never till this day   144
  Saw I him touched with anger so distempered.

PROSPERO
  You do look, my son, in a moved sort,   146
  As if you were dismayed. Be cheerful, sir.
  Our revels now are ended. These our actors,   148
  As I foretold you, were all spirits and
  Are melted into air, into thin air;
  And, like the baseless fabric of this vision,   151
  The cloud-capped towers, the gorgeous palaces,
  The solemn temples, the great globe itself,   153
  Yea, all which it inherit, shall dissolve,   154
  And, like this insubstantial pageant faded,
  Leave not a rack behind. We are such stuff   156
  As dreams are made on, and our little life   157
  Is rounded with a sleep. Sir, I am vexed.   158
  Bear with my weakness. My old brain is troubled.
  Be not disturbed with my infirmity.   160
  If you be pleased, retire into my cell   161
  And there repose. A turn or two I'll walk
  To still my beating mind.

FERDINAND, MIRANDA   We wish your peace.   163

164 **with a thought** i.e., on the instant, or, summoned by my thought, no sooner thought of than here.

165 **cleave** cling, adhere

167 **presented** acted the part of, or, introduced

174 **bending** aiming

176 **unbacked** unbroken, unridden

177 **Advanced** lifted up

178 **As** as if

179 **lowing** mooing

180 **furzes . . . gorse** prickly shrubs

182 **filthy-mantled** covered with a slimy coating

184 **O'erstunk** smelled worse than, or, caused to stink terribly

Exeunt [Ferdinand and Miranda].

PROSPERO

Come with a thought! I thank thee, Ariel. Come.   164

Enter Ariel.

ARIEL

Thy thoughts I cleave to. What's thy pleasure?

PROSPERO   Spirit,   165
We must prepare to meet with Caliban.

ARIEL

Ay, my commander. When I presented Ceres,   167
I thought to have told thee of it, but I feared
Lest I might anger thee.

PROSPERO

Say again, where didst thou leave these varlets?

ARIEL

I told you, sir, they were red-hot with drinking;
So full of valor that they smote the air
For breathing in their faces, beat the ground
For kissing of their feet; yet always bending   174
Towards their project. Then I beat my tabor,
At which, like unbacked colts, they pricked their ears, 176
Advanced their eyelids, lifted up their noses   177
As they smelt music. So I charmed their ears   178
That calflike they my lowing followed through   179
Toothed briers, sharp furzes, pricking gorse, and
     thorns,   180
Which entered their frail shins. At last I left them
I'th' filthy-mantled pool beyond your cell,   182
There dancing up to th' chins, that the foul lake
O'erstunk their feet.

PROSPERO   This was well done, my bird.   184
Thy shape invisible retain thou still.

186 **trumpery** cheap goods, the *glistering apparel* mentioned in the following stage direction

187 **stale** (1) decoy (2) out-of-fashion garments. (With possible further suggestions of "horse piss," as in line 199, and "steal," pronounced like *stale*. For *stale* could also mean "fit for a prostitute.")

192 **cankers** festers, grows malignant.

193 **line** lime tree or linden.

193.1–2 *Prospero and Ariel remain* (The staging is uncertain. They may instead exit here and return with the spirits at line 256.)

198 **jack** (1) knave (2) will-o'-the-wisp

206 **hoodwink this mischance** cover up (literally, blindfold) this mistake.

The trumpery in my house, go bring it hither,   186
For stale to catch these thieves.

ARIEL   I go, I go.   *Exit.*   187

PROSPERO
A devil, a born devil, on whose nature
Nurture can never stick; on whom my pains,
Humanely taken, all, all lost, quite lost!
And as with age his body uglier grows,
So his mind cankers. I will plague them all,   192
Even to roaring.

> *Enter Ariel, loaden with glistering apparel, etc.*

                    Come, hang them on this line.   193

> [*Ariel hangs up the showy finery; Prospero and
> Ariel remain, invisible.*] *Enter Caliban, Stephano,
> and Trinculo, all wet.*

CALIBAN
Pray you, tread softly, that the blind mole may
Not hear a foot fall. We now are near his cell.

STEPHANO Monster, your fairy, which you say is a
harmless fairy, has done little better than played the
jack with us.   198

TRINCULO Monster, I do smell all horse piss, at which
my nose is in great indignation.

STEPHANO So is mine. Do you hear, monster? If I
should take a displeasure against you, look you—

TRINCULO Thou wert but a lost monster.

CALIBAN
Good my lord, give me thy favor still.
Be patient, for the prize I'll bring thee to
Shall hoodwink this mischance. Therefore speak
   softly.   206
All's hushed as midnight yet.

213–14 **o'er ears** over my ears in the filthy horse pond (line 182)

222 **King . . . peer** (Alludes to the old ballad beginning, "King Stephen was a worthy peer.")

227 **frippery** second-hand-clothing shop. (Trinculo knows that what they have just found is much finer.)

231 **The dropsy drown** (An oath. *Dropsy* is a disease characterized by the accumulation of fluid in the connective tissue of the body.)

232 **luggage** cumbersome trash.

234 **crown** head

236 **Mistress line** (Addressed to the linden or lime tree upon which, at line 193, Ariel hung the *glistering apparel*.)

237 **jerkin** jacket made of leather

TRINCULO Ay, but to lose our bottles in the pool—

STEPHANO There is not only disgrace and dishonor in
that, monster, but an infinite loss.

TRINCULO That's more to me than my wetting. Yet this
is your harmless fairy, monster!

STEPHANO I will fetch off my bottle, though I be o'er   213
ears for my labor.   214

CALIBAN
Prithee, my king, be quiet. See'st thou here,
This is the mouth o'th' cell. No noise, and enter.
Do that good mischief which may make this island
Thine own forever, and I thy Caliban
For aye thy footlicker.

STEPHANO Give me thy hand. I do begin to have bloody
thoughts.

TRINCULO [seeing the finery] O King Stephano! O peer!   222
O worthy Stephano! Look what a wardrobe here is
for thee!

CALIBAN
Let it alone, thou fool, it is but trash.

TRINCULO Oho, monster! We know what belongs to a
frippery. O King Stephano!   [He puts on a gown.]   227

STEPHANO Put off that gown, Trinculo. By this hand,
I'll have that gown.

TRINCULO Thy Grace shall have it.

CALIBAN
The dropsy drown this fool! What do you mean   231
To dote thus on such luggage? Let't alone   232
And do the murder first. If he awake,
From toe to crown he'll fill our skins with pinches,   234
Make us strange stuff.

STEPHANO Be you quiet, monster.—Mistress line, is   236
not this my jerkin? [He takes it down.] Now is the jerkin 237

238 **under the line** under the lime tree. (With punning
sense of being south of the equinoctial line or equator;
sailors on long voyages to the southern regions were
popularly supposed to lose their hair from scurvy or
other diseases. Stephano also quibbles bawdily on losing hair through syphilis, and puns in *Mistress* and
jerkin.)   **like** likely

239 **bald** (1) hairless, napless (2) meager

240 **Do, do!** i.e., Bravo! (Said in response to the jesting or
to the taking of the jerkin, or both.)   **steal . . . level**
i.e., steal by means of plumb line and carpenter's level,
methodically. (With put on *line*, "lime tree," line 238,
and *steal*, pronounced like *stale*, i.e., prostitute, contin-
uing Stephano's bawdy quibble.)   **an't like** if it
please

245 **pass of pate** sally of wit. (The metaphor is from
fencing.)

247 **lime** birdlime, sticky substance (to give Caliban sticky
fingers)

250 **barnacles** barnacle geese, formerly supposed to be
hatched from barnacles attached to trees or to rotting
timber; here, evidently used, like *apes*, as types of sim-
pletons

251 **villainous** vilely

252 **lay to** start using

253 **this** i.e., the *glistering apparel*.   **hogshead** large cask

254 **Go to** (An expression of exhortation or remon-
strance.)

261 **dry convulsions** racking cramps

262 **agèd** characteristic of old age

under the line. Now, jerkin, you are like to lose your   238
hair and prove a bald jerkin.   239

TRINCULO   Do, do! We steal by line and level, an't like 240
Your Grace.

STEPHANO   I thank thee for that jest. Here's a garment
for't. [*He gives a garment.*] Wit shall not go unrewarded
while I am king of this country. "Steal by line and
level" is an excellent pass of pate. There's another   245
garment for't.

TRINCULO   Monster, come, put some lime upon your   247
fingers, and away with the rest.

CALIBAN
I will have none on't. We shall lose our time,
And all be turned to barnacles, or to apes   250
With foreheads villainous low.   251

STEPHANO   Monster, lay to your fingers. Help to bear   252
this away where my hogshead of wine is, or I'll turn   253
you out of my kingdom. Go to, carry this.   254

TRINCULO   And this.

STEPHANO   Ay, and this.

       [*They load Caliban with more and more garments.*]

       *A noise of hunters heard. Enter divers spirits, in
       shape of dogs and hounds, hunting them about,
       Prospero and Ariel setting them on.*

PROSPERO   Hey, Mountain, hey!

ARIEL   Silver! There it goes, Silver!

PROSPERO   Fury, Fury! There, Tyrant, there! Hark! Hark!
       [*Caliban, Stephano, and Trinculo are driven out.*]
Go, charge my goblins that they grind their joints
With dry convulsions, shorten up their sinews   261
With agèd cramps, and more pinch-spotted make
   them   262

263 **pard** panther or leopard.   **cat o' mountain** wildcat.

264 **soundly** severely.

267 **little** little while longer

5.1 *Location: Before Prospero's cell.*

2 **crack** collapse, fail. (The metaphor is probably alchemical, as in *project* and *gather to a head*, line 1.)

3 **his carriage** its burden. (Time is no longer heavily burdened and so can go *upright*, standing straight and unimpeded.)

4 **On** Approaching

10 **line grove** grove of lime trees.   **weather-fends** protects from the weather

11 **your release** you release them.

12 **distracted** out of their wits

17 **eaves of reeds** thatched roofs.

Than pard or cat o' mountain.

ARIEL   Hark, they roar!   263

PROSPERO

Let them be hunted soundly. At this hour   264
Lies at my mercy all mine enemies.
Shortly shall all my labors end, and thou
Shalt have the air at freedom. For a little   267
Follow, and do me service.   *Exeunt.*

5.1 ❧ *Enter Prospero in his magic robes, [with his
          staff,] and Ariel.*

PROSPERO

Now does my project gather to a head.
My charms crack not, my spirits obey, and Time   2
Goes upright with his carriage. How's the day?   3

ARIEL

On the sixth hour, at which time, my lord,   4
You said our work should cease.

PROSPERO   I did say so,
When first I raised the tempest. Say, my spirit,
How fares the King and 's followers?

ARIEL   Confined together
In the same fashion as you gave in charge,
Just as you left them; all prisoners, sir,
In the line grove which weather-fends your cell.   10
They cannot budge till your release. The King,   11
His brother, and yours abide all three distracted,   12
And the remainder mourning over them,
Brim full of sorrow and dismay; but chiefly
Him that you termed, sir, the good old lord,
          Gonzalo.
His tears runs down his beard like winter's drops
From eaves of reeds. Your charm so strongly works
          'em   17

18 **affections** disposition, feelings

21 **touch** sense, apprehension

23–4 **that . . . they** I who experience human passions as acutely as they

24 **kindlier** (1) more sympathetically (2) more naturally, humanly

27 **rarer** nobler

33 **Ye . . . groves** (This passage, down through line 50, is an embellished paraphrase of Golding's translation of Ovid's *Metamorphoses*, 7.197–219.)

36 **demi-puppets** puppets of half size, i.e., elves and fairies

37 **green sour ringlets** fairy rings, circles in grass (actually produced by mushrooms)

39 **midnight   mushrooms** mushrooms   appearing overnight

40 **curfew** evening bell, usually rung at nine o'clock, ushering in the time when spirits are abroad

41 **Weak masters** i.e., subordinate spirits, as in 4.1.35

43 **the azured vault** i.e., the sky

That if you now beheld them your affections   18
Would become tender.

PROSPERO   Dost thou think so, spirit?

ARIEL
Mine would, sir, were I human.

PROSPERO   And mine shall.
Hast thou, which art but air, a touch, a feeling   21
Of their afflictions, and shall not myself,
One of their kind, that relish all as sharply   23
Passion as they, be kindlier moved than thou art?   24
Though with their high wrongs I am struck to th'
   quick,
Yet with my nobler reason 'gainst my fury
Do I take part. The rarer action is   27
In virtue than in vengeance. They being penitent,
The sole drift of my purpose doth extend
Not a frown further. Go release them, Ariel.
My charms I'll break, their senses I'll restore,
And they shall be themselves.

ARIEL   I'll fetch them, sir.

                                        Exit.

        [*Prospero traces a charmed circle with his staff.*]

PROSPERO
Ye elves of hills, brooks, standing lakes, and groves,   33
And ye that on the sands with printless foot
Do chase the ebbing Neptune, and do fly him
When he comes back; you demi-puppets that   36
By moonshine do the green sour ringlets make,   37
Whereof the ewe not bites; and you whose pastime
Is to make midnight mushrooms, that rejoice   39
To hear the solemn curfew; by whose aid,   40
Weak masters though ye be, I have bedimmed   41
The noontide sun, called forth the mutinous winds,
And twixt the green sea and the azured vault   43

44-5 **to . . . fire** I have discharged the dread rattling thunderbolt

45 **rifted** riven, split.　**oak** a tree that was sacred to Jove

46 **bolt** thunderbolt

47 **spurs** roots

50 **rough** violent

51 **required** demanded

53 **their senses that** the senses of those whom

58 **air** song.　**and** i.e., which is

59 **fancy** imagination

60 **boiled** i.e., extremely agitated

63 **sociable** sympathetic.　**show** appearance

64 **Fall** let fall

67 **ignorant fumes** fumes that render them incapable of comprehension.　**mantle** envelop

68 **clearer** growing clearer

70 **pay thy graces** requite your favors and virtues

Set roaring war; to the dread rattling thunder   44
Have I given fire, and rifted Jove's stout oak   45
With his own bolt; the strong-based promontory   46
Have I made shake, and by the spurs plucked up   47
The pine and cedar; graves at my command
Have waked their sleepers, oped, and let 'em forth
By my so potent art. But this rough magic   50
I here abjure, and when I have required   51
Some heavenly music—which even now I do—
To work mine end upon their senses that   53
This airy charm is for, I'll break my staff,
Bury it certain fathoms in the earth,
And deeper than did ever plummet sound
I'll drown my book.   *Solemn music*.

> *Here enters Ariel before; then Alonso, with a*
> *frantic gesture, attended by Gonzalo; Sebastian and*
> *Antonio in like manner, attended by Adrian and*
> *Francisco. They all enter the circle which Prospero*
> *had made, and there stand charmed; which*
> *Prospero observing, speaks:*

[*To Alonso*] A solemn air, and the best comforter   58
To an unsettled fancy, cure thy brains,   59
Now useless, boiled within thy skull! [*To Sebastian*
    and Antonio] There stand,   60
For you are spell-stopped.—
Holy Gonzalo, honorable man,
Mine eyes, e'en sociable to the show of thine,   63
Fall fellowly drops. [*Aside*] The charm dissolves
    apace,   64
And as the morning steals upon the night,
Melting the darkness, so their rising senses
Begin to chase the ignorant fumes that mantle   67
Their clearer reason.—O good Gonzalo,   68
My true preserver, and a loyal sir
To him thou follow'st! I will pay thy graces   70

71 **Home** fully

73 **furtherer** accomplice

74 **pinched** punished, afflicted

76 **remorse and nature** pity and natural feeling.
whom you who

81 **reasonable shore** shores of reason, i.e., minds. (Their
reason returns, like the incoming tide.)

85 **discase** disrobe

86 **As . . . Milan** in my former appearance as Duke of
Milan.

90 **couch** lie

92 **After summer** following summer as it moves to various parts of the world

96 **So, so, so** (Expresses approval of Ariel's help as valet.)

Home both in word and deed.—Most cruelly   71
Didst thou, Alonso, use me and my daughter.
Thy brother was a furtherer in the act.—   73
Thou art pinched for't now, Sebastian. [*To Antonio*]
     Flesh and blood,   74
You, brother mine, that entertained ambition,
Expelled remorse and nature, whom, with Sebastian,   76
Whose inward pinches therefore are most strong,
Would here have killed your king, I do forgive thee,
Unnatural though thou art.—Their understanding
Begins to swell, and the approaching tide
Will shortly fill the reasonable shore   81
That now lies foul and muddy. Not one of them
That yet looks on me, or would know me.—Ariel,
Fetch me the hat and rapier in my cell.

          [*Ariel goes to the cell and returns immediately.*]

I will discase me and myself present   85
As I was sometime Milan. Quickly, spirit!   86
Thou shalt ere long be free.

                    Ariel sings and helps to attire him.

ARIEL

          Where the bee sucks, there suck I.
          In a cowslip's bell I lie;
          There I couch when owls do cry.   90
          On the bat's back I do fly
          After summer merrily.   92
        Merrily, merrily shall I live now
        Under the blossom that hangs on the bough.

PROSPERO

     Why, that's my dainty Ariel! I shall miss thee,
     But yet thou shalt have freedom. So, so, so.   96
     To the King's ship, invisible as thou art!
     There shalt thou find the mariners asleep
     Under the hatches. The Master and the Boatswain

101 **presently** immediately

103 **Or ere** before

106 **fearful** frightening

112 **trifle** trick of magic.   **abuse** deceive

113 **late** lately

116 **crave** require

117 **An . . . all** if this is actually happening.   **story** i.e., explanation.

118 **Thy . . . resign** (Alonso made arrangement with Antonio at the time of Prospero's banishment for Milan to pay tribute to Naples; see 1.2.113–27.)

119 **wrongs** wrongdoings.

121 **thine age** your venerable self

124 **subtleties** illusions, magical powers. (Playing on the idea of "pastries, concoctions.")

Being awake, enforce them to this place,
And presently, I prithee.   101

ARIEL
I drink the air before me, and return
Or ere your pulse twice beat.   *Exit.*   103

GONZALO
All torment, trouble, wonder, and amazement
Inhabits here. Some heavenly power guide us
Out of this fearful country!

PROSPERO   Behold, sir King,   106
The wrongèd Duke of Milan, Prospero.
For more assurance that a living prince
Does now speak to thee, I embrace thy body;
And to thee and thy company I bid
A hearty welcome.   [*Embracing him.*]

ALONSO   Whe'er thou be'st he or no,
Or some enchanted trifle to abuse me,   112
As late I have been, I not know. Thy pulse   113
Beats as of flesh and blood; and, since I saw thee,
Th' affliction of my mind amends, with which
I fear a madness held me. This must crave—   116
An if this be at all—a most strange story.   117
Thy dukedom I resign, and do entreat   118
Thou pardon me my wrongs. But how should
     Prospero   119
Be living, and be here?

PROSPERO [*to Gonzalo*]   First, noble friend,
Let me embrace thine age, whose honor cannot   121
Be measured or confined.   [*Embracing him.*]

GONZALO   Whether this be
Or be not, I'll not swear.

PROSPERO   You do yet taste
Some subtleties o'th'isle, that will not let you   124
Believe things certain. Welcome, my friends all!

126 **brace** pair

128 **justify you** prove you to be

136 **whom** we who

139 **woe** sorry

143 **sovereign** efficacious

145 **late** recent

145–7 **and supportable . . . you** and I have much weaker means to make my loss supportable than you can call upon to comfort you

[*Aside to Sebastian and Antonio*] But you, my brace of
    lords, were I so minded,   126
I here could pluck His Highness' frown upon you
And justify you traitors. At this time   128
I will tell no tales.

SEBASTIAN   The devil speaks in him.

PROSPERO   No.
[*To Antonio*] For you, most wicked sir, whom to call
    brother
Would even infect my mouth, I do forgive
Thy rankest fault—all of them; and require
My dukedom of thee, which perforce I know
Thou must restore.

ALONSO   If thou be'st Prospero,
Give us particulars of thy preservation,
How thou hast met us here, whom three hours since   136
Were wrecked upon this shore; where I have lost—
How sharp the point of this remembrance is!—
My dear son Ferdinand.

PROSPERO   I am woe for't, sir.   139

ALONSO
Irreparable is the loss, and Patience
Says it is past her cure.

PROSPERO   I rather think
You have not sought her help, of whose soft grace
For the like loss I have her sovereign aid   143
And rest myself content.

ALONSO   You the like loss?

PROSPERO
As great to me as late, and supportable   145
To make the dear loss, have I means much weaker   146
Than you may call to comfort you; for I   147
Have lost my daughter.

ALONSO   A daughter?

151–3 **That . . . lies** I would wish myself buried in that muddy bed where my son's body lies drowned if that would somehow make them alive and reigning in Naples.

155 **admire** wonder

156 **devour their reason** i.e., are openmouthed, dumbfounded

156–8 **and scarce . . . breath** and scarcely can believe their eyes or their own words.

161 **of** from

164 **of day by day** requiring days to tell, or covering a long span of time

168 **abroad** anywhere else.

170 **requite** repay

172.1 *discovers* i.e., by opening a curtain, presumably rearstage

173 **play me false** cheat.

176–7 **Yes . . . play** i.e., Yes, even if we were playing for twenty kingdoms, something less than the whole world, you would still press your advantage against me, and I would lovingly let you do it as though it were fair play.

O heavens, that they were living both in Naples,
The king and queen there! That they were, I wish   151
Myself were mudded in that oozy bed   152
Where my son lies. When did you lose your daughter? 153

PROSPERO
In this last tempest. I perceive these lords
At this encounter do so much admire   155
That they devour their reason and scarce think   156
Their eyes do offices of truth, their words   157
Are natural breath. But, howsoever you have   158
Been jostled from your senses, know for certain
That I am Prospero and that very duke
Which was thrust forth of Milan, who most strangely 161
Upon this shore, where you were wrecked, was
    landed
To be the lord on't. No more yet of this,
For 'tis a chronicle of day by day,   164
Not a relation for a breakfast nor
Befitting this first meeting. Welcome, sir.
This cell's my court. Here have I few attendants,
And subjects none abroad. Pray you, look in.   168
My dukedom since you have given me again,
I will requite you with as good a thing,   170
At least bring forth a wonder to content ye
As much as me my dukedom.   172

Here Prospero discovers Ferdinand and Miranda,
playing at chess.

MIRANDA   Sweet lord, you play me false.   173

FERDINAND   No, my dearest love,
I would not for the world.

MIRANDA
Yes, for a score of kingdoms you should wrangle,   176
And I would call it fair play.

ALONSO   If this prove   177

178 **vision** illusion
182 **compass** encompass, embrace
185 **brave** splendid, gorgeously appareled, handsome
188 **eld'st** longest

A vision of the island, one dear son   178
Shall I twice lose.

SEBASTIAN   A most high miracle!

FERDINAND [*approaching his father*]
Though the seas threaten, they are merciful;
I have cursed them without cause.   [*He kneels.*]

ALONSO   Now all the blessings
Of a glad father compass thee about!   182
Arise, and say how thou cam'st here.

                    [*Ferdinand rises.*]

MIRANDA   Oh, wonder!
How many goodly creatures are there here!
How beauteous mankind is! Oh, brave new world   185
That has such people in't!

PROSPERO   'Tis new to thee.

ALONSO
What is this maid with whom thou wast at play?
Your eld'st acquaintance cannot be three hours.   188
Is she the goddess that hath severed us,
And brought us thus together?

FERDINAND   Sir, she is mortal;
But by immortal Providence she's mine.
I chose her when I could not ask my father
For his advice, nor thought I had one. She
Is daughter to this famous Duke of Milan,
Of whom so often I have heard renown,
But never saw before; of whom I have
Received a second life; and second father
This lady makes him to me.

ALONSO   I am hers.
But oh, how oddly will it sound that I
Must ask my child forgiveness!

PROSPERO   There, sir, stop.

202 **heaviness** sadness.   **inly** inwardly

205 **chalked . . . way** marked as with a piece of chalk the pathway

207 **Was Milan** Was the Duke of Milan.   **issue** child

214–15 **all . . . own** all of us have found ourselves and our sanity when we all had lost our senses.

216 **still** always.   **his** that person's

220 **blasphemy** i.e., blasphemer

221 **That swear'st grace o'erboard** i.e., you who expel heavenly grace from the ship by your blasphemies. **not an oath** aren't you going to swear an oath

225 **glasses** hourglasses.   **gave out split** reported shipwrecked, gave up for lost

Let us not burden our remembrances with
A heaviness that's gone.

GONZALO   I have inly wept,   202
Or should have spoke ere this. Look down, you gods,
And on this couple drop a blessèd crown!
For it is you that have chalked forth the way   205
Which brought us hither.

ALONSO   I say amen, Gonzalo!

GONZALO
Was Milan thrust from Milan, that his issue   207
Should become kings of Naples? Oh, rejoice
Beyond a common joy, and set it down
With gold on lasting pillars: in one voyage
Did Claribel her husband find at Tunis,
And Ferdinand, her brother, found a wife
Where he himself was lost; Prospero his dukedom
In a poor isle; and all of us ourselves   214
When no man was his own.

ALONSO [to Ferdinand and Miranda]   Give me your hands. 215
Let grief and sorrow still embrace his heart   216
That doth not wish you joy!

GONZALO   Be it so! Amen!

        Enter Ariel, with the Master and Boatswain
        amazedly following.

Oh, look, sir, look, sir! Here is more of us.
I prophesied, if a gallows were on land,
This fellow could not drown.—Now, blasphemy,   220
That swear'st grace o'erboard, not an oath on shore?   221
Hast thou no mouth by land? What is the news?

BOATSWAIN
The best news is that we have safely found
Our King and company; the next, our ship—
Which, but three glasses since, we gave out split—   225

226 **yare** ready.   **bravely** splendidly

228 **tricksy** ingenious, sportive

229 **strengthen** increase

232 **dead of sleep** deep in sleep

234 **several** diverse

240 **Cap'ring to eye** dancing for joy to see.   **On a trice** In an instant

241 **them** i.e., the other crew members

242 **moping** in a daze

246 **conduct** director

248 **infest** harass, disturb.   **beating on** worrying about

249 **picked** chosen, convenient

250 **single** privately.   **resolve** satisfy, explain to

Is tight and yare and bravely rigged as when   226
We first put out to sea.

ARIEL [*aside to Prospero*]   Sir, all this service
Have I done since I went.

PROSPERO [*aside to Ariel*]   My tricksy spirit!   228

ALONSO
These are not natural events; they strengthen   229
From strange to stranger. Say, how came you hither?

BOATSWAIN
If I did think, sir, I were well awake,
I'd strive to tell you. We were dead of sleep,   232
And—how we know not—all clapped under hatches,
Where but even now, with strange and several noises   234
Of roaring, shrieking, howling, jingling chains,
And more diversity of sounds, all horrible,
We were awaked; straightway at liberty;
Where we, in all her trim, freshly beheld
Our royal, good, and gallant ship, our Master
Cap'ring to eye her. On a trice, so please you,   240
Even in a dream, were we divided from them   241
And were brought moping hither.

ARIEL [*aside to Prospero*]   Was't well done?   242

PROSPERO [*aside to Ariel*]
Bravely, my diligence. Thou shalt be free.

ALONSO
This is as strange a maze as e'er men trod,
And there is in this business more than nature
Was ever conduct of. Some oracle   246
Must rectify our knowledge.

PROSPERO   Sir, my liege,
Do not infest your mind with beating on   248
The strangeness of this business. At picked leisure,   249
Which shall be shortly, single I'll resolve you,   250

251 **probable** plausible

251–2 **of every These** about every one of these

252 **accidents** occurrences

253 **well** favorably.

257 **odd** unaccounted for

258–9 **Every . . . himself** (Stephano drunkenly inverts the saying "Every man for himself.")

259–60 *Coraggio* **. . . monster** Have courage, gallant monster

261 **true spies** accurate observers (i.e., sharp eyes)

263 **brave** handsome

264 **fine** splendidly attired

270 **badges** emblems worn by servants to indicate whom they serve

271 **say . . . true** say if they are worthy and loyal servants.

274 **And . . . power** and usurp the moon's command (over tides) without her authority. (Sycorax could control the moon and hence the tides.)

276 **bastard** counterfeit

Which to you shall seem probable, of every   251
These happened accidents; till when, be cheerful   252
And think of each thing well. [*Aside to Ariel*] Come
  hither, spirit.   253
Set Caliban and his companions free.
Untie the spell.   [*Exit Ariel.*]
    [*To Alonso*] How fares my gracious sir?
There are yet missing of your company
Some few odd lads that you remember not.   257

> *Enter Ariel, driving in Caliban, Stephano, and*
> *Trinculo, in their stolen apparel.*

STEPHANO   Every man shift for all the rest, and let no   258
  man take care for himself; for all is but fortune. *Corag*- 259
  gio, bully monster, *coraggio*!   260

TRINCULO   If these be true spies which I wear in my   261
  head, here's a goodly sight.

CALIBAN
  O Setebos, these be brave spirits indeed!   263
  How fine my master is! I am afraid   264
  He will chastise me.

SEBASTIAN   Ha, ha!
  What things are these, my lord Antonio?
  Will money buy 'em?

ANTONIO   Very like. One of them
  Is a plain fish, and no doubt marketble.

PROSPERO
  Mark but the badges of these men, my lords,   270
  Then say if they be true. This misshapen knave,   271
  His mother was a witch, and one so strong
  That could control the moon, make flows and ebbs,
  And deal in her command without her power.   274
  These three have robbed me, and this demidevil—
  For he's a bastard one—had plotted with them   276
  To take my life. Two of these fellows you

278 **own** acknowledge.

282 **reeling ripe** staggeringly drunk.

283 **gilded 'em** flushed their complexion (from the drink), giving them a ruddy or gilded appearance.

284 **pickle** (1) fix, predicament (2) pickling brine (in this case, horse urine).

287 **flyblowing** i.e., being fouled by fly eggs (from which he is saved by being pickled).

291 **sirrah** (Standard form of address to an inferior, here expressing reprimand.)

292 **sore** (1) tyrannical (2) sorry, inept (3) wracked by pain

297 **trim** prepare, decorate

299 **grace** pardon, favor.

Must know and own. This thing of darkness I   278
Acknowledge mine.

CALIBAN   I shall be pinched to death.

ALONSO
Is not this Stephano, my drunken butler?

SEBASTIAN   He is drunk now. Where had he wine?

ALONSO
And Trinculo is reeling ripe. Where should they   282
Find this grand liquor that hath gilded 'em?   283
[*To Trinculo*] How cam'st thou in this pickle?   284

TRINCULO   I have been in such a pickle since I saw you
last that, I fear me, will never out of my bones. I shall
not fear flyblowing.   287

SEBASTIAN   Why, how now, Stephano?

STEPHANO   Oh, touch me not! I am not Stephano, but a
cramp.

PROSPERO   You'd be king o'the isle, sirrah?   291

STEPHANO   I should have been a sore one, then.   292

ALONSO [*pointing to Caliban*]
This is a strange thing as e'er I looked on.

PROSPERO
He is as disproportioned in his manners
As in his shape.—Go, sirrah, to my cell.
Take with you your companions. As you look
To have my pardon, trim it handsomely.   297

CALIBAN
Ay, that I will; and I'll be wise hereafter
And seek for grace. What a thrice-double ass   299
Was I to take this drunkard for a god
And worship this dull fool!

PROSPERO   Go to. Away!

ALONSO
Hence, and bestow your luggage where you found it.

306 **waste** spend

309 **accidents** occurrences

317 **Take** take effect upon, enchant.   **deliver** declare, relate

319–20 **catch . . . far off** enable you to catch up with the main part of your royal fleet, now afar off en route to Naples. (See 1.2.235–6.)

322 **draw near** i.e., enter my cell.

SEBASTIAN   Or stole it, rather.
              [*Exeunt Caliban, Stephano, and Trinculo.*]

PROSPERO
  Sir, I invite Your Highness and your train
  To my poor cell, where you shall take your rest
  For this one night; which, part of it, I'll waste   306
  With such discourse as, I not doubt, shall make it
  Go quick away: the story of my life,
  And the particular accidents gone by   309
  Since I came to this isle. And in the morn
  I'll bring you to your ship, and so to Naples,
  Where I have hope to see the nuptial
  Of these our dear-belovèd solemnized;
  And thence retire me to my Milan, where
  Every third thought shall be my grave.

ALONSO   I long
  To hear the story of your life, which must
  Take the ear strangely.

PROSPERO   I'll deliver all;   317
  And promise you calm seas, auspicious gales,
  And sail so expeditious that shall catch   319
  Your royal fleet far off. [*Aside to Ariel*] My Ariel, chick,   320
  That is thy charge. Then to the elements
  Be free, and fare thou well!
                  [*To the others*] Please you, draw near.   322
                        Exeunt omnes [except Prospero].

Epilogue.

9 **bands** bonds

10 **hands** i.e., applause (the noise of which could break a charm).

11 **Gentle breath** Favorable breeze (produced by hands clapping or favorable comment)

13 **want** lack

16 **prayer** i.e., Prospero's petition to the audience

17 **assaults** penetrates the heart of

18 **frees** obtains forgiveness for

19 **crimes** sins

20 **indulgence** (1) humoring, lenient approval (2) remission of punishment for sin

Epilogue ✦ *Spoken by* PROSPERO.

Now my charms are all o'erthrown,
And what strength I have 's mine own,
Which is most faint. Now, 'tis true,
I must be here confined by you
Or sent to Naples. Let me not,
Since I have my dukedom got
And pardoned the deceiver, dwell
In this bare island by your spell,
But release me from my bands   9
With the help of your good hands.   10
Gentle breath of yours my sails   11
Must fill, or else my project fails,
Which was to please. Now I want   13
Spirits to enforce, art to enchant,
And my ending is despair,
Unless I be relieved by prayer,   16
Which pierces so that it assaults   17
Mercy itself, and frees all faults.   18
As you from crimes would pardoned be,   19
Let your indulgence set me free.   *Exit.*   20

DATE AND TEXT

The Tempest was first printed in the First Folio of 1623. It occupies first place in the volume and is a scrupulously prepared text from a transcript by Ralph Crane of a theater playbook or of Shakespeare's draft after it had been annotated for production; or, Crane may have provided some of the elaboration of stage directions. Shakespeare's colleagues may have placed *The Tempest* first in the Folio because they considered it his most recent complete play. The first recorded performance was at court on November 1, 1611: "Hallomas nyght was presented att Whithall before ye kinges Maiestie a play Called the Tempest." The actors were "the Kings players" (*Revels Account*). The play was again presented at court during the winter of 1612–1613, this time "before the Princes Highnes the Lady Elizabeth and the Prince Pallatyne Elector." The festivities for this important betrothal and wedding were sumptuous and included at least thirteen other plays. Various arguments have been put forward that Shakespeare composed parts of *The Tempest*, especially the masque, for this occasion, but there is absolutely no evidence that the play was singled out for special prominence among the many plays presented, and the masque is integral to the play as it stands. Probably the 1611 production was of a fairly new play. Simon Forman, who saw *Cymbeline* and *The Winter's Tale* in 1611, does not mention *The Tempest*. He died in September 1611. According to every stylistic test, such as run-on and hypermetric lines, the play is very late. Shakespeare probably knew Sylvester Jourdain's *A Discovery of the Bermudas*, published in 1610, and William Strachey's *A True Reportory of the Wreck and Redemption*, dated July 1610, although not published until 1625.

TEXTUAL NOTES

These textual notes are not a historical collation, either of the early folios or of more recent editions; they are simply a record of departures in this edition from the copy text. The reading adopted in this edition appears in boldface, followed by the rejected reading from the copy text, i.e., the First Folio. Only major alterations in punctuation are noted. Changes in lineation are not indicated, nor are some minor and obvious typographical errors.

Copy text: the First Folio. Characters' names are groups at the heads of scenes throughout. Act and scene divisions are as marked in the Folio.

Names of the Actors [printed in F at the end of the play]

1.1.8.1 Ferdinand *Ferdinando*   **34 s.d. Exeunt** *Exit*   **36** [and elsewhere]   **wi'th'** *with*   **38.1** [at line 37 in F]

1.2.99 exact, like *exact. Like*   **166 steaded much.** *steeded much,*   **174 princes** *Princesse*   **201 bowsprit** *Bore-spritt*   **213 me. The** *me the*   **230 Bermudas** *Bermoothes*   **284 she** *he*   **288 service. Thou** *service, thou*   **330 forth at** *for that*   **377.5, 399.1 Ariel's** *Ariel (or Ariell)*   **385 s.d. Burden, dispersedly** [before Hark, hark!" in line 384 in F]   **387** [F provides a speech prefix, Ar.]   **400 ARIEL** [not in F]

2.1.38 ANTONIO *Seb.*   **39 SEBASTIAN** *Ant.*   **185 mettle** *mettal*   **234 throes** *throwes*

2.2.9 mow *moe*   **116 spirits** *sprights*

3.1.2 sets *set*

3.2.51–2 isle; / From me he *Isle / From me, he*   **123 scout** *cout*

3.3.15 travel *trauaile*   **17.1–2 Solemn . . . invisible** [after "they are fresh" in F, and followed by the s.d. at line 19, *Enter . . . depart*]   **28 me** *me?*   **29 islanders?** *Islands;*   **33 human** *humaine*   **65 plume** *plumbe*

4.1.9 off of   **13 gift** guest   **25 love as 'tis now, the** loue, as 'tis
now the   **61 vetches** Fetches   **68 poll-clipped** pole-clipt
74 Her here   **110 CERES** [not in F]   **124.1–2** [after line 127 in F]
163.1 Exeunt Exit   **193 s.d. Enter Ariel . . . etc.** [after "on this
line" in F, and followed by *Enter* Caliban . . . *all wet*]   **193 them on**
on them   **232 Let't** let's

5.1.60 boiled boile   **72 Didst** Did   **75 entertained** entertaine
82 lies ly   **88 ARIEL** [not in F]   **111 Whe'er** Where
236 horrible, horrible.   **238 her** our   **249 business. At** businesse,
at   **250 Which . . . single** (Which shall be shortly single)
260 *coraggio* Corasio

SHAKESPEARE'S SOURCES

No direct literary source for the whole of *The Tempest* has been found. Shakespeare does seem to have drawn material from various accounts of the shipwreck of the *Sea Venture* in the Bermudas, in 1609, although the importance of these materials should not be overstated. Several of the survivors wrote narratives of the shipwreck itself and of their life on the islands for some nine months. Sylvester Jourdain, in *A Discovery of the Bermudas*, published 1610 (see the selection that follows), speaks of miraculous preservation despite the island's reputation for being "a most prodigious and enchanted place." William Strachey's letter, written in July of 1610 and published much later (1625) as *A True Repertory of the Wreck and Redemption . . . from the Islands of the Bermudas*, describes (as can be seen in the selection that follows) the panic among the passengers and crew, the much-feared reputation of the island as the habitation of devils and wicked spirits, the actual beauty and fertility of the place with its abundance of wild life (cf. Caliban's descriptions), and the treachery of the Indians they later encounter in Virginia. Shakespeare seems to have read Strachey's letter in manuscript and may have been acquainted with him. The storm scene in Chapter 4 of Laurence Twine's *The Pattern of Painful Adventures*, a major source for *Pericles*, may also have given Shakespeare material for the first scene of *The Tempest*; see the source materials in the Bantam edition of that play. Shakespeare also kept up with travel accounts of Sir Water Ralegh and Thomas Harriot, and knew various classical evocations of a New World. The name "Setebos" came from Richard Eden's *History of Travel* (1577) translated from Peter Martyr's *De Novo Orbe* and from other travel accounts of the period. (See the Introduction to the play for the potential relevance of various journals of the circumnavigation of the globe.) All these hints are indeed suggestive, but they are scattered and relate more to the setting and general circumstance of Shakespeare's play than to the plot.

Shakespeare certainly consulted Michel de Montaigne's essay "Of the Cannibals," as translated by John Florio in 1603. Gonzalo's reverie on an ideal commonwealth (2.1.150–171) contains many verbal echoes of the essay, as can be seen in the selection that follows. Montaigne's point is that supposedly civilized persons who condemn as barbarous any society not conforming with their own are simply refusing to examine their own shortcomings. A supposedly primitive society may well embody perfect religion, justice, and harmony; civilized art can never rival the achievements of nature. The ideal commonwealth has no need of magistrates, riches, poverty, and contracts, all of which breed dissimulation and covetousness. The significance of these ideas for The Tempest extends well beyond the particular passage in which they are found. And Caliban himself, whose name is an anagram of "cannibal," illustrates (even though he is not an eater of human flesh) the truth of Montaigne's observation apropos of the intense and wanton cruelty he finds so widespread in so-called Western civilization: "I think there is more barbarism in eating men alive than to feed upon them being dead."

Prospero's famous valedictory speech to "Ye elves of hills, brooks, standing lakes, and groves" (5.1.33–57) owes its origin to Medea's similar invocation in Ovid's Metamorphoses (Book 7), which Shakespeare knew both in the Latin original and in Golding's translation: "Ye airs and winds, ye elves of hills, of brooks, of woods alone, / Of standing lakes . . ." Medea also anticipates Shakespeare's Sycorax. Medea thus provides material for the representation of both black and white magic in The Tempest, so carefully differentiated by Shakespeare. Ariel is part English fairy, like Puck, and part daemon. The pastoral situation in The Tempest is perhaps derived from Edmund Spenser's The Faerie Queene, Book 6 (with its distinctions between savage lust and true courtesy, between nature and art). Italian pastoral drama as practiced by Guarini and (in England) by John Fletcher may also have been an influence. The masque element in *The Tempest*, prominent as in much late Shakespeare, bears the imprint of the courtly masque tradition of Ben Jonson, Francis Beaumont, and Samuel Daniel. Virgil's *Aeneid* may have provided Shakespeare with a more indirect source, with its story of wandering in the Mediterranean and storm at sea, love in Carthage, the intervention of the gods, and the fulfillment of destiny in Italy.

A German play, *Die Schöne Sidea* by Jacob Ayrer, written before 1605, was once thought to have been based on an earlier version of *The Tempest* as performed by English players traveling in Germany. Today the similarities between the two plays are generally attributed to conventions found everywhere in romance.

A DISCOVERY OF THE BERMUDAS

By Sylvester Jourdain

Being in ship called the *Sea Venture*, with Sir Thomas Gates, our governor, Sir George Somers, and Captain Newport, three most worthy honored gentlemen, whose valor and fortitude the world must needs take notice of, and that in most honorable designs bound for Virginia, in the height of thirty degrees of northerly latitude or thereabouts, we were taken with a most sharp and cruel storm upon the five and twentieth day of July, Anno 1609. Which did not only separate us from the residue of our fleet, which were eight in number, but, with the violent working of the seas, our ship became so shaken, torn, and leaked that she received so much water as covered two tier of hogsheads[1] above the ballast, that our men stood up to the middles with buckets, barricos,[2] and kettles to bail out the water and continually pumped for three days and three nights together without any intermission, and yet the water seemed rather to increase than to diminish. Insomuch that all our men, being utterly spent, tired, and disabled for longer labor, were even resolved, without any hope of their lives, to shut up the hatches

1 **hogsheads** large barrels or casks   2 **barricos** kegs

and to have committed themselves to the mercy of the sea (which is said to be merciless) or rather to the mercy of their mighty God and redeemer (whose mercies exceed all his works), seeing no help nor hope in the apprehension of man's reason that any mother's child could escape that inevitable danger which every man had proposed and digested[3] to himself of present[4] sinking.

So that some of them, having some good and comfortable waters[5] in the ship, fetched them and drunk one to the other, taking their last leave one of the other until their more joyful and happy meeting in a more blessed world. When it pleased God, out of his most gracious and merciful providence, so to direct and guide our ship, being left to the mercy of the sea for her most advantage, that Sir George Somers, sitting upon the poop of the ship, where he sat three days and three nights together without meals' meat[6] and little or no sleep, conning[7] the ship to keep her as upright as he could (for otherwise she must needs instantly have foundered),[8] most wishedly happily descried land.

Whereupon he most comfortably encouraged the company to follow[9] their pumping and by no means to cease bailing out of the water with their buckets, barricos, and kettles, whereby they were so over-wearied, and their spirits so spent with long fasting and continuance of their labor, that for the most part they were fallen asleep in corners and wheresoever they chanced first to sit or lie. But hearing news of land, wherewith they grew to be somewhat revived, being carried with will and desire beyond their strength, every man bustled up and gathered his strength and feeble spirits together to perform as much as their weak force would permit him.

Through which weak means it pleased God to work so strongly as[10] the water was stayed[11] for that little time, which, as we all much feared, was the last period of our breathing,[12] and

---

3 digested pondered   4 present immediate   5 waters distilled alcohol
6 meals' meat food   7 conning steering, navigating   8 foundered be engulfed, sent to the bottom   9 follow keep up   10 as that
11 stayed held back   12 the last . . . breathing i.e., our last gasp

the ship kept from present sinking, when it pleased God to send her within half an English mile of that land Sir George Somers had not long before descried—which were the islands of the Bermudas. And there neither did our ship sink, but, more fortunately in so great a misfortune, fell in[13] between two rocks, where she was fast lodged and locked for further budging. Whereby we gained not only sufficient time, with the present help of our boat and skiff, safely to set and convey our men ashore (which were one hundred and fifty in number), but afterwards had time and leisure to save some good part of our goods and provision which the water had not spoiled, with all the tackling[14] of the ship and much of the iron about her, which were necessaries not a little available for the building and furnishing of a new ship and pinnace,[15]* which we made there for the transporting and carrying of us to Virginia.

But our delivery was not more strange in falling so opportunely and happily upon the land as our feeding and preservation was beyond our hopes and all men's expectations most admirable. For the islands of the Bermudas, as every man knoweth that hath heard or read of them, were never inhabited by any Christian or heathen people, but ever esteemed and reputed a most prodigious and enchanted place, affording nothing but gusts, storms, and foul weather, which made every navigator and mariner to avoid them as Scylla and Charybdis,[16] or as they would shun the devil himself; and no man was ever heard to make for[17] the place but as[18] against their wills they have, by storms and dangerousness of the rocks lying seven leagues into the sea, suffered shipwreck. Yet did we find there the air so temperate and the country so abundantly fruitful of all fit necessaries for the sustenation and preservation of man's life, that most in a manner of all[19] our provisions of bread, beer, and

13 **fell in** i.e., steered her way 14 **tackling** ropes and pulleys
15 **pinnace** a light sailing vessel used as a tender for a larger ship
16 **Scylla and Charybdis** monster and whirlpool facing each other across a narrow strait in *The Odyssey*, Book 12 17 **make for** head for
18 **as** that 19 **most in a manner of all** i.e., even though nearly all

victual being quite spoiled in lying long drowned in salt water, notwithstanding we were there for the space of nine months (few days over or under) not only well refreshed, comforted, and with good satiety contented, but, out of the abundance thereof, provided us some reasonable quantity and proportion[20] of provision to carry us for Virginia and to maintain ourselves and that company we found there, to the great relief of them, as it fell out in their so great extremities and in respect of the shortness of time, until it pleased God that, by my lord's[21] coming thither, their store was better supplied. And greater and better provisions we might have had if we had had better means for the storing and transportation thereof. Wherefore my opinion sincerely of this island is that whereas it hath been and is still accounted the most dangerous, infortunate, and most forlorn place of the world, it is in truth the richest, healthfulest, and pleasing land (the quantity and bigness thereof considered) and merely[22] natural as ever man set foot upon.

20 proportion share   **21 my lord's** i.e., Sir Thomas Gates's
22 merely utterly

[Most of the remainder of A Discovery of the Bermudas is taken up with a description of the island, its flora and fauna, etc., much as in William Strachey's account.]

Text based on A Discovery of the Bermudas [spelled Barmudas in the original], Otherwise Called the Isle of Devils, by Sir Thomas Gates, Sir George Somers, and Captain Newport, with Divers Others. . . . London, Printed by John Windet . . . 1610.

In the following, the departure from the original text appears in bold-face; the original reading is in roman.

p. 173 *pinnace pinms

A TRUE REPERTORY OF THE WRECK AND
REDEMPTION OF SIR THOMAS GATES, KNIGHT,
UPON AND FROM THE ISLANDS
OF THE BERMUDAS

By William Strachey

[Strachey's account is in the form of a letter, beginning as the
fleet of seven ships and two pinnaces—i.e., light sailing vessels
used as tenders for the larger ships—is within seven or eight days'
sailing of Cape Henry, Virginia, in late July of 1609.]

When on Saint James his day, July 24, being Monday,
preparing for no less all the black night before, the clouds
gathering thick upon us and the winds singing and whistling
most unusually, which made us to cast off our pinnace, towing
the same until then astern, a dreadful storm and hideous
began to blow from out the northeast, which, swelling and
roaring as it were by fits, some hours with more violence than
others, at length did beat all light from heaven; which like
an hell of darkness turned black upon us, so much the more
fuller of horror as in such cases horror and fear use to[1] overrun
the troubled and overmastered senses of all, which, taken up
with amazement, the ears lay so sensible to the terrible cries
and murmurs of the winds and distraction of our company as
who was most armed[2] and best prepared was not a little
shaken. . . .

For four and twenty hours the storm in a restless tumult had
blown so exceedingly as we could not apprehend in our imagi-
nations any possibility of greater violence. Yet did we still find it
not only more terrible but more constant, fury added to fury and
one storm urging a second more outrageous than the former,
whether it so wrought upon our fears or indeed met with new

1 use to habitually, characteristically   2 as who was most armed that
even that person who was most ready to protect himself

forces. Sometimes shrieks[3]* in our ship amongst women and
passengers not used to such hurly and discomforts made us look
one upon the other with troubled hearts and panting bosoms.
Our clamors drowned in the winds, and the winds in thunder.
Prayers might well be in the heart and lips, but drowned in the
outcries of the officers. Nothing heard that could give comfort,
nothing seen that might encourage hope.

It is impossible for me, had I the voice of Stentor[4] and expression of as many tongues as his throat of voices, to express the
outcries and miseries. . . . In which the sea swelled above the
clouds and gave battle unto heaven. It could not be said to rain;
the waters like whole rivers did flood in the air. And this I did
still observe: that whereas upon the land, when a storm hath
poured itself forth once in drifts of rain, the wind, as beaten
down and vanquished therewith, not long after endureth; here
the glut of water, as if throttling the wind erewhile,[5] was no
sooner a little emptied and qualified but instantly the winds, as
having gotten their mouths now free and at liberty, spake more
loud and grew more tumultuous and malignant.

What shall I say? Winds and seas were as mad as fury and
rage could make them. For mine own part, I had been in some
storms before. . . . Yet all that I had ever suffered gathered together might not hold comparison with this. There was not a
moment in which the sudden splitting or instant oversetting of
the ship was not expected.

Howbeit, this was not all. It pleased God to bring a greater
affliction yet upon us, for in the beginning of the storm we had
received likewise a mighty leak. And the ship . . . was grown five
foot suddenly deep with water above her ballast, and we almost
drowned within whilst we sat looking when to perish from
above. This, imparting no less terror than danger, ran through
the whole ship with much fright and amazement, startled and
turned the blood and took down the braves[6] of the most hardy

3 **shrieks** (The original *strikes* is probably an error for *shrikes*.)
4 **Stentor** a Greek with a voice as loud as fifty men   5 **erewhile** formerly   6 **braves** courage

mariner of them all, insomuch as he that before happily felt not the sorrow of others now began to sorrow for himself when he saw such a pond of water so suddenly broken in, and which he knew could not, without present avoiding, but instantly sink him. . . .

Once, so huge a sea brake upon the poop and quarter upon us, as it covered our ship from stern to stem like a garment or a vast cloud; it filled her brim full for a while within, from the hatches up to the spar deck. This source, or confluence, of water was so violent as[7] it rushed and carried the helmsman from the helm and wrested the whipstaff[8] out of his hand, which so flew from side to side that, when he would have seized[9] the same again, it so tossed him from starboard to larboard as it was God's mercy it had not split him. It so beat him from his hold and so bruised him as[10] a fresh man, hazarding in by chance, fell fair with it and, by main strength bearing somewhat up, made good his place,[11] and with much clamor encouraged and called upon others, who gave her now up, rent in pieces and absolutely lost. . . .

During all this time, the heavens looked so black upon us that it was not possible the elevation of the pole might be observed,[12] nor a star by night nor sunbeam by day was to be seen. Only upon the Thursday night, Sir George Somers, being upon the watch, had an apparition of a little round light, like a faint star, trembling and streaming along with a sparkling blaze half the height upon the mainmast and shooting sometimes from shroud to shroud, tempting[13] to settle as it were upon any of the four shrouds. And for three or four hours together, or rather more, half the night it kept with us, running sometimes along

---

7 **as** that   8. **whipstaff** handle attached to the tiller   9 **seized** i.e., secured, stopped its uncontrolled whipping about   10 **as** that   11 **made good his place** (Another seaman, coming on the scene by chance, managed by brute strength to secure the tiller and its handle.) **made good** supplied   12 **the elevation . . . observed** to measure the elevation of the polestar above the horizon (and thereby determine latitude)   13 **tempting** attempting. (The phenomenon observed is St. Elmo's fire, as in *The Tempest*, 1.2.197–202.)

the mainyard to the very end and then returning. At which Sir George Somers called divers about him and showed them the same, who observed it with much wonder and carefulness. But upon a sudden, towards the morning watch, they lost the sight of it and knew not what way it made. The superstitious seamen make many constructions of this sea fire, which nevertheless is usual in storms—the same, it may be, which the Grecians were wont in the Mediterranean to call Castor and Pollux, of which, if one only appeared without the other, they took it for an evil sign of great tempest.[14] The Italians and such, who lie open to the Adriatic and Tyrrhene Sea,[15] call it a sacred body, *Corpo sancto*. The Spaniards call it Saint Elmo, and have an authentic and miraculous legend for it. Be it what it will, we laid other foundations of safety or ruin than in the rising or falling of it. Could it have served us now miraculously to have taken our height by,[16] it might have strucken amazement and a reverence in our devotions, according to the due of a miracle. But it did not light us any whit the more to our known way, who ran now (as do hoodwinked men) at all adventures,[17] sometimes north and northeast, then north and by west . . . and sometimes half the compass. . . .

It being now Friday, the fourth morning, it wanted little but that there had been[18] a general determination to have shut up hatches, and, commending our sinful souls to God, committed the ship to the mercy of the sea. Surely that night we must have done it, and that night had we then perished. But see the goodness and sweet introduction of better hope by our merciful God given unto us! Sir George Somers, when no man dreamed of such happiness, had discovered and cried[19] land. . . . But having

14 Castor and Pollux . . . tempest (This name, taken from the twin sons of Tyndarus and Leda, was applied to St. Elmo's fire because, when the phenomenon appeared in pairs simultaneously, it was thought to signal the cessation of a storm.)   15 Tyrrhene Sea Tyrrhenian Sea, lying between Italy, Sicily, and Sardinia   16 to have . . . by to have measured our latitude by. (See note 12 above.)   17 at all adventures totally at random   18 it wanted . . . been i.e., we were very close to. it wanted there lacked   19 cried announced, called out

no hope to save her by coming to an anchor in the same [some smooth water under the southeast point of the land], we were enforced to run her ashore as near the land as we could, which brought us within three quarters of a mile of shore; and, by the mercy of God unto us, making out our boats,[20] we had ere night brought all our men, women, and children—about the number of one hundred and fifty—safe into the island.

We found it to be the dangerous and dreaded island, or rather islands, of the Bermuda, whereof let me give Your Ladyship[21] a brief description before I proceed to my narration. And that the rather,[22] because they be so terrible to all that ever touched on them, and such tempests, thunders, and other fearful objects are seen and heard about them that they be called commonly the Devil's Islands, and are feared and avoided of all sea travelers alive above any other place in the world. Yet it pleased our merciful God to make even this hideous and hated place both the place of our safety and means of our deliverance.

And hereby also I hope to deliver the world from a foul and general error, it being counted[23] of most that they can be no habitation for men, but rather given over to devils and wicked spirits. Whereas indeed we find them now by experience to be as habitable and commodious as most countries of the same climate and situation, insomuch as, if the entrance into them were as easy as the place itself is contenting, it had long ere this been inhabited as well as other islands. Thus shall we make it appear that Truth is the daughter of Time, and that men ought not to deny everything which is not subject to their own sense.

[Strachey proceeds with a description of the islands—their climate, topography, flora and fauna, etc.]

Sure it is that there are no rivers nor running springs of fresh water to be found upon any of them. When we came first, we

20 **making out our boats** setting out our small ship's boats   21 **Your Ladyship** the noble lady to whom the letter is written   22 **rather** sooner   23 **counted** reckoned, supposed

digged and found certain gushings and soft bubblings which, being either in bottoms or on the side of hanging ground, were only fed with rain water which nevertheless soon sinketh into the earth and vanisheth away, or emptieth itself out of sight into the sea without any channel above or upon the superficies[24] of the earth. For according as their rains fell, we had wells and pits which we digged either half full or absolute exhausted and dry; howbeit some low bottoms, which the continual descent from the hills filled full, and in those flats could have no passage away, we found to continue as fishing ponds or standing pools, continually summer and winter full of fresh water.

The shore and bays round about when we landed first afforded great store of fish, and that of divers kinds, and good. . . . We have taken also from under the broken rocks crevices[25] oftentimes greater than any of our best English lobsters, and likewise abundance of crabs, oyster, and whelks. True it is, for fish in every cove and creek we found snaules and skulles[26] in that abundance as I think no island in the world may have greater store or better fish. . . .

Fowl there is great store. . . . A kind of webfooted fowl there is, of the bigness of an English green plover or seamew,[27] which all the summer we saw not, and in the darkest nights of November and December (for in the night they only feed) they would come forth but not fly far from home and, hovering in the air and over the sea, made a strange hollow and harsh howling. . . . Our men found a pretty way to take them, which was by standing on the rocks or sands by the seaside and halooing, laughing, and making the strangest outcry that possibly they could. With the noise whereof the birds would come flocking to that place and settle upon the very arms and head of him that so cried, and still creep nearer and nearer, answering the noise themselves; by which our men would weigh them with their

---

24 superficies surface   **25 crevices** crayfish. (French *écrevisse*.)   **26 snaules and skulles** (Identity uncertain: snails or snailfish and schools or skullfish?)   **27 seamew** sea gull (perhaps to be identified with the *scamels* mentioned by Caliban in *The Tempest*, 2.2.170)

hand, and which weighed heaviest they took for the best and let the others alone, and so our men would take twenty dozen in two hours of the chiefest of them; and they were a good and well-relished fowl, fat and full as a partridge.

[Among the other adventures reported by Strachey is a conspiracy or mutiny aimed at the life of their governor, but the leaders are apprehended. Later, when they reach Virginia and find the colony of Jamestown in a perilous state, the voyagers encounter some native Indians and are surprised to discover "how little a fair and noble entreaty works upon a barbarous disposition."]

Strachey's letter, written in 1610, was published as *A True Repertory of the Wreck and Redemption of Sir Thomas Gates, Knight, upon and from the Islands of the Bermudas, His Coming to Virginia, and the Estate of the Colony Then and After under the Government of the Lord La Warre. July, 15, 1610, written by William Strachey, Esquire.* In Samuel Purchas, *Purchas His Pilgrims* (1625), Part 4, Book 9, Chapter 6, pp. 1734 ff.

In the following, the departure from the original text appears in boldface; the original reading is in roman.

p. 176 *shrieks strikes

THE ESSAYS OF MICHAEL, LORD OF MONTAIGNE

Translated by John Florio

BOOK I, CHAPTER 30: OF THE CANNIBALS

[Montaigne begins by citing approvingly the opinion of King Pyrrhus of Greece that the so-called barbarians are often far from barbarous. "Lo, how a man ought to take heed lest he overweeningly follow vulgar opinions, which should be measured by the rule of reason and not by the common report." Montaigne cites various examples and then turns to the American Indians.]

Now, to return to my purpose, I find (as far as I have been informed) there is nothing in that nation that is either barbarous or savage, unless men call that barbarism which is not common to them. As indeed we have no other aim of truth and reason than the example and idea of the opinions and customs of the country we live in. There is ever perfect religion, perfect policy,[1] perfect and complete use of all things. They[2] are even "savage" as we call those fruits wild which nature of herself and of her ordinary progress[3] hath produced, whereas indeed they are those which ourselves have altered by our artificial devices and diverted from their common order we should rather term "savage."[4] In those[5] are the true and most profitable virtues and natural properties most lively and vigorous, which in these[6] we have bastardized, applying them to the pleasure of our corrupted taste. And if, notwithstanding, in divers fruits of those countries that were never tilled we shall find that, in respect of[7] ours, they are most excellent and as delicate unto our taste, there is no reason art should gain the point of honor of[8] our great and puissant mother Nature. We have so much by our inventions surcharged[9] the beauties and riches of her works that we have altogether overchoked her; yet wherever her purity shineth, she makes our vain and frivolous enterprises wonderfully ashamed.

> *Et veniunt hederae sponte sua melius,*
> *Surgit et in solis formosior arbutu antris,*
> *Et volucres nulla dulcius arte canunt.*
> [Propertius]

1 **There . . . policy** i.e., There, in our own society as we complacently view it, is always perfect religion, perfect government   2 **They** i.e., Those "savage" people   3 **progress** course, way   4 **they are those . . . "savage"** we should instead term "savage" those things we ourselves have artificially diverted from their natural function.   5 **those** i.e., things made by nature   6 **these** i.e., things diverted by us from their natural function   7 **in respect of** in comparison with   8 **should . . . honor of** should be awarded the prize over   9 **by our inventions surcharged** by means of our artificial contrivances overwhelmed

> Ivies spring better of their own accord;
> Unhaunted[10] plots much fairer trees afford;
> Birds by no art much sweeter notes record.

All our endeavors or wit cannot so much as reach to represent the nest of the least birdlet, its contexture, beauty, profit, and use, no, nor the web of a silly[11] spider. "All things," saith Plato, "are produced either by nature, by fortune, or by art. The greatest and fairest by one or other of the two first, the least and imperfect by the last."

Those nations seem therefore so barbarous unto me because they have received very little fashion from human wit[12] and are yet near their original naturality. The laws of nature do yet command them, which are but little bastardized[13] by ours, and that with such purity as I am sometimes grieved the knowledge of it came no sooner to light at what time[14] there were men that better than we could have judged of it. I am sorry Lycurgus[15] and Plato had it not, for me seemeth that, what in those nations we see by experience doth not only exceed all the pictures wherewith licentious[16] poesy hath proudly embellished the golden age and all her quaint inventions to feign[17] a happy condition of man, but also the conception and desire of philosophy. They[18] could not imagine a genuity[19] so pure and simple as we see it by experience,[20] nor ever believe[21] our society might be maintained with so little art and humane combination. It

---

10 Unhaunted unfrequented   **11 silly** innocent, simple, tiny   **12 Those . . . wit** i.e., Those so-called savage nations seem therefore "barbarous" to me only in the sense that they have received little fashioning from civilized intellect   **13 but little bastardized** scarcely diverted from their natural function   **14 at what time** when   **15 Lycurgus** legendary Spartan legislator whose name was applied to important social and legal reforms c. 600 B.C.   **16 licentious** taking free poetic license, playing fast and loose with the truth   **17 all her . . . feign** all of poesy's ingenious fabrications used to imagine or pretend   **18 They** i.e., poesy and philosophy   **19 genuity** ingenuousness, simplicity   **20 by experience** i.e., by looking at the ways of so-called "savage" peoples   **21 believe** believe that

is a nation, would I answer Plato, that hath no kind of traffic,[22] no knowledge of letters,[23] no intelligence[24] of numbers,
no name of magistrate,[25] nor of politic superiority,[26] no use of
service,[27] of riches, or of poverty, no contracts, no successions, no
dividances, no occupation but idle,[28] no respect of kindred but
common,[29] no apparel but natural, no manuring of lands, no
use of wine, corn,[30] or metal. The very words that import lying,
falsehood, treason, dissimulations, covetousness, envy, detraction,[31] and pardon, were never heard of amongst them. How
dissonant would he find[32] his imaginary commonwealth from this
perfection!

> Hos natura modos primum dedit.

> Nature at first uprise[33]
> These manners did devise.
>   [Virgil]

Furthermore, they live in a country of so exceeding pleasant
and temperate situation that, as my testimonies[34] have told me,
it is very rare to see a sick body amongst them; and they have
further assured me they never saw any man there either shaking
with the palsy, toothless, with eyes dropping,[35] or crooked and
stooping through age.

[Montaigne continues with a description of their abundance.
Later in the essay he examines cannibalism in the same rela-
tivistic terms:]

22 **traffic** trade   23 **letters** writing   24 **intelligence** knowledge,
science   25 **of magistrate** for a magistrate   26 **politic superiority**
political hierarchy   27 **service** servitude   28 **but idle** except leisure
ones   29 **no respect . . . common** no kinship ties except those held
in common   30 **corn** wheat. (Grains grown naturally, not by agri-
culture.)   31 **detraction** belittling   32 **How dissonant would he
find** i.e., How far (from this ideal state of affairs) would he, Plato, find
33 **at first uprise** at her very beginnings   34 **testimonies** witnesses
35 **with eyes dropping** i.e., bleary-eyed or discharging fluid

I am not sorry we note the barbarous horror of such an action, but grieved that, prying so narrowly into their faults, we are so blinded in ours. I think there is more barbarism in eating men alive than to feed upon them being dead—to mangle by tortures and torments a body full of lively sense,[36] to roast him in pieces, to make dogs and swine to gnaw and tear him in mammocks[37] (as we have not only read but seen very lately, yea, and in our own memory, not amongst ancient enemies but our neighbors and fellow citizens, and, which is worse, under pretense and piety and religion) than to roast and tear him after he is dead.

36 lively sense acute feeling   **37 mammocks** shreds

Text based on *The Essays, or Moral, Politic, and Military Discourses of Lord Michael de Montaigne. . . . First written by him in French. And now done into English by . . . John Florio. Printed at London by Val. Sims for Edward Blount . . . 1603.*

METAMORPHOSES

By Ovid
Translated by Arthur Golding

BOOK 7

[Medea, preparing to use her magical powers to prolong the life of Jason's father, Aeson, invokes the spirits of the unseen world.]

Ye airs and winds, ye elves of hills, of brooks, of
    woods alone,
Of standing lakes, and of the night, approach ye
    everychone!   266
Through help of whom, the crooked banks much
    wondering at the thing,
I have compellèd streams to run clean backward to
    their spring.

266 everychone everyone

By charms I make the calm seas rough and make the
    rough seas plain,
And cover all the sky with clouds and chase them
    thence again.
By charms I raise and lay the winds, and burst the
    viper's jaw,   271
And from the bowels of the earth both stones and
    trees do draw.
Whole woods and forests I remove; I make the
    mountains shake,
And even the earth itself to groan and fearfully to
    quake.
I call up dead men from their graves; and thee, O
    lightsome Moon,   275
I darken oft, though beaten brass abate thy peril
    soon.   276
Our sorcery dims the morning fair and darks the sun
    at noon.

271 lay allay, cause to subside   **275 lightsome** light-giving   **276
though . . . soon** (Alludes to the belief that a loud noise such as that
produced by beating on metal would frighten away the malign influence
of an eclipse.)

Text based on *The XV Books of P. Ovidius Naso, Entitled Metamorphoses.
Translated out of Latin into English meter by Arthur Golding, Gentleman. A
work very pleasant and delectable. . . . Imprinted at London by William
Seres. 1567.*

FURTHER READING

Auden, W. H. "The Sea and the Mirror: A Commentary on Shakespeare's *The Tempest.*" *For the Time Being.* New York: Random House, 1944. Rpt. in *The Collected Poetry of W. H. Auden.* New York: Random House, 1945. Auden's "The Sea and the Mirror" is a poetic meditation on *The Tempest*, a sequence of imagined speeches taking up where Shakespeare's play ends. Characters declare their new knowledge of what they are: Antonio still recalcitrant, Prospero poignantly aware of his own limitations, and Caliban voicing the disturbing reality that he represents for both Prospero and the audience.

Brockbank, J. Philip. "*The Tempest:* Conventions of Art and Empire." *Later Shakespeare*, ed. John Russell Brown and Bernard Harris. Stratford-upon-Avon Studies 8. London: Edward Arnold; New York: St. Martin's, 1966. In the accounts of the wreck of the *Sea Venture* and the miraculous survival of its crew, Brockbank finds the origins of *The Tempest's* emphasis upon providential control and moral change. For him the play celebrates the process of conversion and repentance, not in the organic metaphors of seasonal growth as in Shakespeare's pastoral plays, but in images of the mysterious, renewing action of the sea.

Coleridge, Samuel Taylor. "*The Tempest.*" *Coleridge's Writings on Shakespeare*, ed. Terence Hawkes. New York: G. P. Putnam's Sons, 1959. In a series of lectures, Coleridge discusses the "astonishing and intuitive knowledge" of character that Shakespeare reveals in "this, almost miraculous, drama." Ariel is a spirit of the air, necessarily resenting that "he is bound to obey Prospero." Caliban "is all earth," but Shakespeare "has raised him far above contempt." Of Prospero and Miranda Coleridge says: "I have often thought of Shakespeare as the mighty wizard himself introducing as the first and fairest pledge of his so potent art, the female character in all its charms. . . ."

Coursen, H. R. "*The Tempest*": *A Guide to the Play.* Westport, Conn., and London: Greenwood Press, 2000. Coursen provides a sensible and useful introduction to *The Tempest*, with readable essays on the play's textual history, its sources, structure, and themes, and its critical and performance history.

Felperin, Howard. "Undream'd Shores: *The Tempest*." *Shakespearean Romance*. Princeton, N.J.: Princeton Univ. Press, 1972. Romance, according to Felperin, is both the subject and the genre of *The Tempest*. The play tests the ability of the imagination to perfect reality, and if Prospero's magic is ultimately found unable to reconcile the idealizing impulses of romance and the resistances of history, Shakespeare's art can—in the play's ingenious combination of a fictional political action and a romantic account of a shipwreck based on historical sources.

Fiedler, Leslie A. "The New World Savage as Stranger; or, ' 'Tis New to Thee.' " *The Stranger in Shakespeare*. New York: Stein and Day, 1972. In a provocative reading of the play focusing on its relation to the colonizing enterprise of Renaissance Europe, Fiedler argues that Caliban's role as "a savage and deformed slave" reveals the inadequacy of the play's twin utopian hopes: Gonzalo's vision of an idealized political existence and Prospero's fantasy of innocent love.

Frey, Charles. "*The Tempest* and the New World." *Shakespeare Quarterly* 30 (1979): 29–41. Believing the play to be neither "an autonomous imaginative construct" nor "an historical document," Frey suggestively examines accounts of Sir Francis Drake's circumnavigation of the globe and records of the Jamestown settlement to explore *The Tempest*'s "peculiar merger of history and romance."

Frye, Northrop. *A Natural Perspective: The Development of Shakespeare's Comedy and Romance*, passim. New York: Columbia Univ. Press, 1965. Frye treats the late romances as a return to and culmination of the logic of the earlier romantic comedies. In *The Tempest* Frye discovers the comic movement from confusion to identity and from sterility to renewed life, lifting us out of the world of ordinary experience into a world perfected by the human imagination.

Henderson, Diana E. "*The Tempest* in Performance." *Companion to Shakespeare's Works: The Poems, Problem Plays, Late Plays*, ed. Richard Dutton and Jean E. Howard. Oxford: Blackwell, 2003. Henderson begins a sensitive and subtle essay by asking "What does *The Tempest* perform?" She decides that the narrative of

Prospero's revenge cannot account for the critical and theatrical energy that surrounds the play. By examining the performance history of the play (including its many adaptations), she shows how the play exceeds its own narrative, becoming a "meta-event" for critics and directors, that is, an occasion to consider any of "the many issues suggested by the characters in their imaginary terrain."

Hulme, Peter, and William H. Sherman, eds. *"The Tempest" and Its Travels*. Philadelphia: University of Pennsylvania Press, 2000. A remarkable, rich, and provocative anthology of critical essays and poems, play scenes, and visual images inspired by Shakespeare's play. The essays were commissioned for the volume, and they focus on the play as a rhetorical structure, a theatrical event, and a document of seventeenth-century England. There is a particular focus on the new-world contexts of the play and on the modern receptions and rewritings of it in the Americas.

James, Henry. "Introduction to *The Tempest*." *Complete Works of Shakespeare*, 1907, ed. Sydney Lazarus Lee. Rpt. in *Henry James: Selected Literary Criticism*, ed. Morris Shapiro. London: Heineman, 1963; New York: Horizon, 1964. In his introduction to *The Tempest*—one of "the supreme works of all literature"— James reflects upon the contradiction between the man who, having written the play, retires to Stratford, and the artist at the peak of his powers of expression, aware of his mastery of style and characterization.

Kermode, Frank. *"The Tempest." William Shakespeare: The Final Plays*. London: Longmans, Green, 1963. While *The Tempest*, like Shakespeare's other late plays, develops the familiar themes of repentance and renewal, its handling of this romantic material differs from the others in the neoclassic design of the plot and the philosophical and spectacular elements drawn from the masque. Above all, for Kermode, the play is strange and elusive, lacking the other romances' sustained notes of joy and rising above the ingenuities of criticism that would contain its mystery.

Kernan, Alvin B. " 'The Great Globe Itself': The Public Playhouse and the Ideal Theater of *The Tempest*." *The Playwright as Magician: Shakespeare's Image of the Poet in the English Public Theater*. New Haven, Conn.: Yale Univ. Press, 1979. Kernan finds that in the creation and control of Prospero's island kingdom through art lie Shakespeare's strongest claims for the power of the theatrical imagination: the play is both visionary and moral, re-creating in Prospero's suffering and exile the central pattern of existence.

Kott, Jan. "Prospero's Staff." *Shakespeare Our Contemporary*, trans. Boleslaw Taborski. Garden City, N.Y.: Doubleday, 1964. In Kott's dark vision of *The Tempest,* the island is not a utopian landscape but a stage on which the history of the world with its endless struggles for power is elementally enacted. Prospero's rule over Caliban's island mirrors Antonio's usurpation of Prospero's throne; Sebastian's hope to murder Alonso repeats Antonio's fratricidal desires; and the plot of Stephano, Trinculo, and Caliban to depose and murder Prospero farcically reenacts all of the grim human history that Kott sees centrally reflected in the play.

Marx, Leo. "Shakespeare's American Fable." *The Machine in the Garden: Technology and the Pastoral Ideal in America*. London and New York: Oxford Univ. Press, 1964. Marx argues that the early European travel narratives envisioning the New World either as an earthly paradise or a hideous wilderness generate the poles of *The Tempest's* dialectical treatment of nature and civilization. The final affirmations of the play, he argues, rest on the successful mediation of this opposition, as Prospero learns both the necessity of his art to control and shape fallen nature and the limitations of his art to perfect it.

Nostbakken, Faith. *Understanding "The Tempest": A Student Casebook to Issues, Sources and Historical Documents*. Westport, Conn., and London: Greenwood Press, 2004. Nostbakken brackets a valuable collection of historical documents (on magic, race, colonialism, and Renaissance courts), reviews of various productions of the play, and excerpts from critical studies with her own essay on the play's setting, characters, and dramatic development, and a set of "Contemporary Applications," which relate the play to political issues of our time and also compare Shakespeare's use of fantasy with that of the popular fiction of Tolkien and Rowling.

Orgel, Stephen. "New Uses of Adversity: Tragic Experience in *The Tempest*." *In Defense of Reading: A Reader's Approach to Literary Criticism*, ed. Reuben A. Brower and Richard Poirier.

New York: E. P. Dutton, 1962; rpt. in *Essays in Shakespearean Criticism*, ed. James L. Calderwood and Harold E. Toliver. Englewood Cliffs, N.J.: Prentice-Hall, 1970. Examining the play's movement toward harmony, Orgel discovers the power and authority of the redemptive action in the experience of tragedy. Prospero leads the characters through suffering to reconciliation, not denying but transforming tragedy in the shifts of perspective achieved by his art. Even in the happy end, however, the tragic implications of human nature are not evaded as Prospero leaves the island and his magic for the imperfect world of human society.

Summers, Joseph H. "The Anger of Prospero." *Dreams of Love and Power*. Oxford: Clarendon Press, 1984. Examining the various scenes in which Prospero appears irritated or angry, Summers discovers the cause in Prospero's anxiety about both his own responsibility for the past and his ability to shape the future to the happy end he desires. Only when the play's complex harmonies have been achieved and Prospero is without power is he also without anger.

Sundelson, David. "So Rare a Wonder'd Father: Prospero's *Tempest*." *Representing Shakespeare: New Psychoanalytic Essays*, ed. Murray M. Schwartz and Coppélia Kahn. Baltimore: Johns Hopkins Univ. Press, 1980. Rev. and rpt. in *Shakespeare's Restorations of the Father*. New Brunswick, N.J.: Rutgers Univ. Press, 1983. Sundelson brings the vocabulary and concerns of psychoanalytic criticism to *The Tempest*, locating the play's central concerns in its complex representation of fatherhood. He traces the articulated anxieties about power and sexuality and examines the process by which Prospero masters these, making possible the play's final harmony in his altruistic surrender to the desires of others.

Vaughan, Virginia Mason, and Alden Vaughan, eds. *Critical Essays on Shakespeare's "The Tempest."* New York: G. K. Hall, 1998. A useful anthology of contemporary scholarship on the sources of the play, its staging, and its major ideational concerns, including magic and colonialism, in essays by, among others, Jonathan Bate, Meredith Skura, Barbara Mowat, Russ McDonald, and Ann Thompson.

MEMORABLE LINES

❧

Methinks he hath no drowning mark upon him; his
complexion is perfect gallows. (GONZALO 1.1.29–31)

               What see'st thou else
In the dark backward and abysm of time? (PROSPERO 1.2.49–50)

Your tale, sir, would cure deafness. (MIRANDA 1.2.106)

          . . . my library
Was dukedom large enough. (PROSPERO 1.2.109–10)

From the still-vexed Bermudas . . . (ARIEL 1.2.230)

You taught me language, and my profit on't
Is I know how to curse. The red plague rid you
For learning me your language! (CALIBAN 1.2.366–8)

This music crept by me upon the waters,
Allaying both their fury and my passion
With its sweet air. (FERDINAND 1.2.395–7)

[*Song*]   Full fathom five thy father lies.
   Of his bones are coral made.
Those are pearls that were his eyes.
   Nothing of him that doth fade
But doth suffer a sea change
Into something rich and strange. (ARIEL 1.2.400–5)

. . . lest too light winning
Make the prize light. (PROSPERO 1.2.455–6)

There's nothing ill can dwell in such a temple.
If the ill spirit have so fair a house,
Good things will strive to dwell with't. (MIRANDA 1.2.461–3)

He receives comfort like cold porridge. (SEBASTIAN 2.1.10–11)

I'th commonwealth I would by contraries
Execute all things; for no kind of traffic
Would I admit; no name of magistrate . . . (GONZALO 2.1.150–2)

. . . nature should bring forth,
Of it own kind, all foison, all abundance,
To feed my innocent people.   (GONZALO 2.1.165–7)

What's past is prologue.   (ANTONIO 2.1.254)

Misery acquaints a man with strange bedfellows.
          (TRINCULO 2.2.39–40)

I prithee, let me bring thee where crabs grow,
And I with my long nails will dig thee pignuts.
          (CALIBAN 2.2.165–6)

[*Song*]   'Ban, 'Ban, Ca—Caliban
Has a new master. Get a new man!   (CALIBAN 2.2.182–3)

Be not afeard. The isle is full of noises,
Sounds, and sweet airs, that give delight and hurt not.
          (CALIBAN 3.2.137–8)

                    Do not give dalliance
Too much the rein.   (PROSPERO 4.1.51–2)

Our revels now are ended. These our actors,
As I foretold you, were all spirits and
Are melted into air, into thin air.   (PROSPERO 4.1.148–50)

                    We are such stuff
As dreams are made on, and our little life
Is rounded with a sleep.   (PROSPERO 4.1.156–8)

A devil, a born devil, on whose nature
Nurture can never stick.   (PROSPERO 4.1.188–9)

                    I have bedimmed
The noontide sun, called forth the mutinous winds,
And twixt the green sea and the azured vault
Set roaring war.   (PROSPERO 5.1.41–4)

                    Graves at my command
Have waked their sleepers, oped, and let 'em forth
By my so potent art.   (PROSPERO 5.1.48–50)

[*Song*]   Where the bee sucks, there suck I.
In a cowslip's bell I lie;
There I couch when owls do cry.
On the bat's back I do fly.   (ARIEL 5.1.88–91)

                    Oh, brave new world
That has such people in't!   (MIRANDA 5.1.185–6)

                    This thing of darkness I
Acknowledge mine.   (PROSPERO 5.1.278–9)

                    Then to the elements
Be free, and fare thou well!   (PROSPERO 5.1.321–2)